A Beginner's Guide
to the Path
of Ascension

Joshua David Stone, Ph.D.

A Beginner's Guide to the Path of Ascension

Joshua David Stone, Ph.D.
and Rev. Janna Shelley Parker

THE EASY-TO-READ ENCYCLOPEDIA of the SPIRITUAL PATH
✦ Volume VII ✦

Published by
Light Technology Publishing

Cover design by
Fay Richards

ISBN 1-891824-02-3

Published by
Light Technology Publishing
P.O. Box 1526
Sedona, AZ 86339
(800) 450-0985

Printed by
MISSION POSSIBLE
Commercial Printing
P.O. Box 1495
Sedona, AZ 86339

Note

Message from Joshua David Stone
For the sake of clarity, this book has been written
using the pronoun "I" even though there are two authors.
I think the book reads much easier this way.

Special Thank-Yous

I extend a special thank-you to another wonderful spiritual sister, Mary Rosales, for her devoted and selfless computer work, which allowed the logistical aspect of putting this book together to occur at lightning speed.

I also acknowledge Michael Day for his outstanding editing help. His joy, love, enthusiasm, skill and devotion to his work are greatly appreciated.

Contents

Introduction

In order to understand the true meaning of "ascension" and all that the term implies, one must first begin with an understanding of the basic nature of man. Most humans sense that they are more than flesh and bone, more than emotions, more than minds. But unless one has consciously delved into mystical and occult studies, he/she is left a bit lost at sea with these vague feelings. The intent of this book, therefore, is to define man's spiritual components in order that the reader may more easily comprehend the great spiritual truths that are part of each and every one of us. Likewise, this information is intended to reveal the nature of humanity in relationship to the various kingdoms coexisting upon this beloved planet to the higher spiritual kingdoms with which humans interact daily and to the glorious and divine destiny that awaits humanity via the forces within evolution itself and humanity's conscious progress along the path of ascension.

There is more and more material available on the subject of ascension. However, it occurs to me that in order for this material to be of greatest service one must first be acquainted with the essential divine make-up of humanity, building a solid base from which to view humans as the spiritual beings they are—a sort of launching pad for one's cosmic voyage of ascension. Therefore, this book is dedicated to those who are first consciously waking up to realms they are already subconsciously or superconsciously aware of, but nevertheless need to consciously understand. This book is likewise dedicated to the many who are well on their way along the path of ascension, but who might like a few of the missing steps of understanding filled in. In truth, this book is most properly dedicated to the seeking minds and hearts of all humans, who, like children eager for a favorite bedtime story, never tire of hearing the telling and retelling of the cosmic and divine destiny that awaits us all.

I hope that those who are newly awakened buds upon the tree of spirituality and ascension can, with the aid of this book, more easily blossom into the maturity of their divine selves by welcoming into their minds the higher vision of themselves. I likewise hope that those who are better acquainted with the initiation and ascension process and with a more comprehensive understanding of the true nature of their beings will take the time to share this book with friends. And it is my fervent wish that even the most well-versed readers of occult studies will find herein another lens through which to observe their spiritual process, finding room to incorporate some of the basic understandings that have been perhaps glossed over as they made their ascension "leaps" from one phase of development to the next.

Last but certainly not least, this book is dedicated to the Spiritual Hierarchy themselves, without whose divine guidance we would all be stumbling about in near darkness, searching for a candle to light the way. And to all the great ones who have lighted our candles by the flame of their own and who have shone as brilliant suns to bring us forward into the daylight of our understanding, do I humbly extend my gratitude and thanks, for they reveal to each of us the glory that we too shall someday be.

1

Humanity As Spiritual Beings
(on the Path of Evolution and Ascension)
Our Spiritual Selves

To begin with, man does not simply *have* a soul—man *is* the soul that inhabits the various bodies (the different bodies I will momentarily address). From an even higher perspective (beyond soul) man is spirit, a divine spark of that which we call God. And it is this spirit that manifests as soul, which then incarnates upon the Earth in order to grow, evolve, expand and ultimately return home to spirit or God, bringing with it upon its return the unique individuality and spiritual treasures it has accumulated through its process of reincarnation in the material worlds.

Therefore, let us proceed with the assumption that humanity does indeed reincarnate, using each incarnation to experience and ultimately master the various bodies. Reincarnation is indeed fact, and the process of sequential births is inextricably interwoven with the development of the physical/etheric, psychic/feeling or emotional/astral and mental bodies. For the sake of simplification I shall refer to them as the four lower bodies: the physical, etheric, astral and mental bodies. We have higher spiritual bodies as well, and I shall discuss them later.

The Physical Body

The physical body is the most familiar of the four lower bodies, since it's the one we see daily and the one that first meets the eye. Also familiar are the five senses with which we process the external world. These five senses—sight, hearing, smell, taste and touch—constitute the most immediate way we interact with the world. But equally obvious is the fact that these senses cannot be separated from our thought or feeling world because we all use the entire four-body system to process the world around us (although we might not be aware of this).

The Etheric Body

Before proceeding to the astral body, which is the body form of the feeling world, I must draw attention to the etheric body, which is a subtler counterpart to the physical body. The etheric body interpenetrates (as do all the bodies) the physical body and can be likened to a blueprint of the physical. Many healers use the images from this body to diagnose difficulties within the physical body. It is this form that is most often seen departing the physical body immediately after death. It is via the connection to this body that an amputee feels what is called phantom pain after the removal of a limb. In this case, what is being felt is the reality of the perfect blueprint of that limb and mentally transferring the pain of the loss to the etheric double of that limb, which suddenly finds itself without a physical point of connection. Of course, the etheric limb itself feels no pain. The etheric body also connects, in a more subtle fashion, to the etheric bodies and to the world at large through subtle energy links. Much, though by no means all, of the aura can be seen by psychics who are able to perceive the emanations of the etheric form.

The Astral Body

The astral body comprises the sensory and emotional world of each individual. It also interpenetrates the physical body and the etheric body. Looking at the planet as a whole, one who is able to do so could see the astral body of Earth herself. It includes the full spectrum of feelings and emotions ranging from animalistic greed and violence to the most sublime emanations of devotion, love and beatitude.

There have been people throughout humanity's evolution so clairvoyantly gifted that they could actually perceive these feelings taking on literal shape and color. On a more practical level, when police find themselves at a standstill in investigations they sometimes hire psychics—gifted people able to pick up often quite-detailed impressions from an article of clothing or object that bears the *astral imprint* of either the victim or perpetrator of a crime. This process is known as *psychometry*.

Many are familiar with the experience of walking into a room and feeling a warm, welcoming embrace or a cold, even malevolent presence. Extreme negativity of feeling can and does leave its mark, and most of us are sensitive to this to some degree. Likewise, the tranquil emanations of a church or other place of spiritual devotion fills our hearts—sometimes to the extent that simply entering a place can so profoundly touch us that our eyes well with sudden tears.

The Mental Body

The same is true of the mental body and thought atmosphere of ourselves individually and our world collectively. This body penetrates the physical, etheric and astral and is of a higher frequency than the others. However, in the four-body system of man these bodies combine to form a cohesive whole. Thought is a very powerful aspect of ourselves and, through steady and concentrated focus, can help bring forth into manifestation that which seems out of reach on the physical level. "Thoughts are things," said Edgar Cayce, and he could not have been more on the mark. Certain clairvoyants have likewise seen the images of thoughts in the same manner as they have seen the images of feelings. There is a distinct shape, size, and form to what we think, and we wear our thoughts about us in much the same manner as we wear our clothing, but thoughts are made of a more enduring substance.

All things start with thoughts. Everything first proceeds out of mind and then is acted upon, taking solidity and manifestation upon the physical plane. Without thought, humanity would not be a separate kingdom from that of the animals, for it is the very substance of mind that denotes a human being.

Again, psychics are often employed to tune in to the thought world of a case that eludes traditional investigative measures because since thoughts are a substance unto themselves, they can see things that are not visible to normal eyes. People who are developed in reading mental auras can easily see into the mental world of another. However, they should never abuse this gift by invading privacy or for selfish reasons.

Looked at more deeply, we can see how we are all sensitive to the thoughts around us. When entering an environment that holds dark thoughts, we frequently pick up on these images—much as a phonograph needle picks up sounds recorded long ago—and we are either repelled by or, sometimes, drawn into them. The power of thought combined with the astral/emotional bodies taken en masse is vast indeed, and it is the strong mental and astral emanations that make many of us so vulnerable to mass hysteria, riots and so forth.

Synopsis

For these reasons the path of ascension requires us to be master of our four-body systems, so that we may act as cocreators with God rather than reacting as victims of those less developed than ourselves. From one viewpoint, it can be said that the path of ascension is in the raising or ascending of the energies of these four bodies into their higher aspects, which are light and love—and thus reflective of the divine.

This brief synopsis of the four lower bodies gives but the barest glimpse into the vastness we will explore in greater depth. It does, however, offer us the sounding line we need to go further.

The key points to remember are that man/woman does not simply have a soul, but rather *is* the soul and ultimately the spirit that inhabits the four-body system during reincarnation upon the planes of matter. We enter into the incarnation process with these bodies barely formed, and through many births and deaths, evolve these bodies both individually and as an entire planet.

Humanity is now at a point in which the development of the planet is great enough to see many souls beginning to raise the frequencies of these bodies, first, by the forces of evolution itself and, second, by virtue of the efforts individuals have put into the process of self-mastery. This has led many through various initiations or expansions into more divine frequencies of light and love. The transformation that occurs is called ascension, in that those operating at lower frequencies are now raised up as to have their soul/spirits ascend to the frequency of God.

All this shall be discussed in detail. However, first I offer you this simple sketch of the four-body system in relationship to humanity's process of using it to gain the experience to grow, evolve, master self and progress along the path of initiation and ascension back to God.

More on Our Spiritual Selves—the Higher Bodies

Now I offer the broader picture of the higher bodies, which are also functioning and evolving. I will not go into great depth and detail, but rather give a simple overview of the aspects of ourselves that are the soul, oversoul and monad.

The Monadic Body

Each of us is basically spirit, or *monad*. This is our God-self, from which we, as souls, first spring forth. A simple way to look at this is found in the words of Jesus Christ in the New Testament: "No one shall go unto the Father lest they first come from the Father." This particular statement has been shrouded in mystery, but it is actually stating an occult fact.

What Jesus is saying is that we all come forth from spirit, or monad—that part of ourselves which is ever at one with the One, or God. And it is indeed our divine destiny to return to that spiritual state from whence we first came forth in order to become cocreators with God.

The spirit, or monad (as I shall proceed to call it), has its home upon the monadic plane of being. The monadic plane is one of the highest planes of being, which from a very much higher frequency interpenetrates and/or incorporates the other planes (such as the physical, astral, mental) within its sphere. It is one of the highest planes of the body within which we live, move and have our being. The frequency of the monadic part of ourselves is so high that in order for it to enter into the lower worlds, it must first create vehicles, or bodies, for those worlds.

The Soul Body

The body most closely related to the monadic is called the oversoul in occult literature, otherwise known as the higher self. This, for purposes of this discussion, is the higher soul family to which we belong. Our individual souls spring forth from this oversoul or soul family and hence we have the individual personality, who, life and after life, incarnates and reincarnates upon the physical, etheric, astral and mental worlds in order to evolve and build up the soul body with the divine attributes of love, light, tenderness, harmlessness, service, devotion and so forth.

The home of the oversoul is upon the buddhic plane, which, again, is a plane like unto the four lower planes mentioned before and falls midway between the monadic plane and the physical plane. Occult writings often refer to the buddhic plane as the causal plane, for it is indeed the plane from which the cause or purpose of our incarnations originates.

Eventually, through the process of reincarnation over vast periods of time, the individualized soul will itself be in direct contact with the monad, sometimes also referred to as the mighty I Am Presence. I mention these phrases because they permeate mystical and occult literature. I have my own phrases of preference but shall continue to present their many variances for a while, so that you may become accustomed to the way in which they are used.

Reincarnation of the Bodies

In summary, what we come from is our God-self, mighty I Am Presence or monad. This divine aspect of our being then creates the oversoul or higher self, which is the basic soul family to which our individual souls belong. Our individual souls are that part of ourselves that follows the process of reincarnation through the rounds of birth and death to evolve and ultimately return to our God-selves or monads (mighty I Am Presence). We do this through the natural course of evolution. Once we assume responsibility for our growth and the cultivation of the divine within ourselves, we, the soul, are on the path of initiation, which leads us to continued conscious growth on our path of ascension. This involves bringing the four lower bodies under the direction of the aforementioned higher aspects (or bodies) of ourselves, which is of utmost importance.

Humanity is not a random accident as many a scientist would have us believe. To the contrary, we must learn to follow the ancient advice to "know ye are gods" and to know as fact and with the fullness of our beings that we are sons and daughters of the most high. To understand ascension, we must first understand that we are indeed created in the image of God, or as the ancient writings of the East tell us in the Bhagavad Gita: "Atman (soul) is Brahmin (God) and that thou art." We are part and parcel of God, ever one with the One, and we are here to grow in both awareness and expression of our divine natures.

For me, reincarnation was something that always seemed to be fact-based. However, I am aware that for the Westerner, this often seems more fancy than fact. For those of the Eastern tradition, the process of reincarnation is common belief. Many of us are aware of the testing that goes on today to determine which child has been reborn as the Dalai Lama. The fact of reincarnation is not at issue, only to find the one soul who is that specific reincarnation. This is so openly written about and accepted in Hindu and Eastern tradition that individual examples would serve only to diffuse the point. What might be interesting to note is that reincarnation was a basic belief within the Jewish and Christian traditions, and was omitted by decree of a certain Pope in relatively recent times.

Examples are to be found all through the New Testament, which still holds much of the basic Jewish belief system within it. For example, people wondered whether John the Baptist was the reincarnation of Elijah. For those who care to reread this book of books, or to explore some of the New Age translations of it, reference upon reference to reincarnation will be made abundantly clear.

Reincarnation is an integral part of understanding the process of ascension and initiation. If it is not already part of your belief system or inner knowing, I do ask that, pending your further investigation, you will proceed to read with an attitude of acceptance in this process, as it is vital to your further understanding of ascension. As with all things, keep an open mind and remember, "there are more things in Heaven and Earth . . . than are dreamt of in your philosophy."

The Spiritual Realms or Planes

I have shared with you, simply as possible, the various bodies in which we, as souls and spirits (or monads), dwell. I have also alluded to the realms or planes where these bodies are to be found. However, the planes and realms themselves merit discussion here.

The realm of matter, the basic physical realm in which humanity daily walks the Earth—the plane where the physical body makes physical contact—is the realm most often called reality. Obviously, this physical plane is but one of several planes of reality, as many of you reading this book will have sensed. Nevertheless, this is the plane most often considered to be reality itself. As we are familiar with this realm, we do not need to examine it except in the light of the other realms, taking into account how the interpretation and energies from these other realms interact with the density of the physical.

The Etheric Realm

The etheric realm interpenetrates, as does the etheric body, and functions as a type of blueprint for the physical realm. However, the etheric realm has a dual purpose and manifestation. Whereas, it is indeed the reflection of the physical world at a higher frequency and in a more perfect form, likewise does it both transmit and absorb various psychic energies issuing forth from the physical realm to the etheric, or from the etheric realm to the physical. By this I mean that a person's aura will permeate this realm, even as it surrounds the person him/herself. It will carry with it the vibrations or energy field of that person, reflecting either a pleasant or unpleasant aura, depending upon what the particular individual both thinks and feels. This takes quite a definite shape upon the etheric plane, and as it interpenetrates the physical, likewise it has the appropriate effect upon all who come in contact with that particular person.

While the higher etheric realms coexist and interpenetrate the physical, they also function as a realm or plane unto themselves. It is upon this realm that many ascended masters (once freed from the rounds of birth and death) might descend and set up a home and teaching center to work with disciples who are incarnated in the physical realms. They do this so that they can be closer to humanity and help uplift us with vibrations of light brought so close to the physical plane as to be but one step above so called reality.

This realm also hosts many devas, etheric beings who tend the plant kingdom and are spoken of in folklore as elves, gnomes and wood sprites. This kingdom, which we shall explore more fully later on, is composed of matter just a bit more refined than that of humanity and is therefore only visible to those with *inner occult vision*. I can assure you that this kingdom and these beings are quite real and are often visible to children, who, in their purity, are not blocked by any prejudice toward the physical realm. As humanity's vision keeps expanding, there are more reports of people seeing and communicating with these wondrous creatures. One of the keys to their world lies in unlocking the door of the heart that love may flow abundantly, for it is through love that this kingdom reveals itself to us. And it is as humanity develops the love nature within that this kingdom will begin to work in greater cooperation with us.

It is worthwhile to repeat that if one wishes to heal him/herself or another, invoking a perfect etheric blueprint will affect the physical body.

Just as the ills of humanity can be seen within the etheric realm, so too can the perfect image and vision be called forth to find its place of manifestation upon the physical form. It is vital to remember that the various realms are connected one to the other in an upward hierarchical fashion, as well as a totally interconnected and interpenetrating one.

One very important point about the etheric realm needs mentioning. Much of humanity's spiritual evolution is charted through the development of the chakras, which are etheric counterparts to certain physical organs and glands. The chakra system is to be found in almost all occult literature, but much of what is written barely scratches the surface of this complex system, which extends throughout all the various realms of being, back to the godhead itself. It is worth offering an overview of the seven basic chakras and important centers.

- Soul star: a bright star about six inches above the head; an extension of the oversoul.
- Top of head: 7th chakra, also known as the thousand-petal lotus when fully functioning. This is likewise seen as the aura drawn or painted around the heads of Christ, the Virgin Mary and saints merged with their God-self.
- Center of head: 6th or third-eye chakra, related to inner vision.
- Throat: 5th chakra; related to the thyroid, creativity, communication and God's will.
- Heart: 4th chakra; related to the expression of unconditional love.
- Solar plexus: 3rd chakra; related to emotions.
- Sacral plexus: 2nd chakra; related to the sexual organs.
- Base of spine: 1st chakra; related to instinctive nature and basic survival.
- Knees
- Soles of feet
- Earth star: About one foot below ground, directly under the feet; serves to link heaven to Earth.

The Astral Realm

The astral realm is a world unto itself. And this world is itself divided into subdivisions, ranging from the lower astral worlds peopled with less-evolved souls through various grades where the more evolved souls dwell between their life cycles. However, for souls to be found among the astral regions, the silver cord that links the soul with the physical body need not be disengaged as it is at the time of so-called death. For these regions are visited at night during the hours of sleep. Therefore, one might accurately say that the astral world is peopled by both incarnate (but sleeping) entities and disincarnate entities (those people who have passed through the portals of death).

The astral realm is much like the physical realm, except that things have a greater luster and vision is of a truer and clearer nature. For example, on Earth one chooses the clothing one wears. On the astral realm one forms clothing out of the nature of one's being, and it cannot help but reflect the inner nature of the person. The many veils with which we struggle on the physical plane to hide ourselves—both from ourselves and each other—are stripped away. And so we stand spiritually naked—revealed as we are.

In a like manner, the communities to which we are drawn are the direct result of the spiritual unfolding of the divine qualities within us. Those who have developed some degree of mastery over the lower animalistic desires and emotions, who have cultivated an appreciation of the arts and peaceful, loving harmony, will be drawn to a community of like souls. And the houses within which they dwell will likewise be reflective of this nature, as well as their entire physical appearance.

There are temples of great learning on the astral realms and many souls, while still in body, visit these universities at night, while others who have left the body will devote much of their time to the study of higher truths in these wonderful places. Many ascended masters choose this higher sphere of the astral planes to conduct these classes and bring forth greater vision to those dwelling upon those planes. Likewise, many disciples and initiates choose to use this realm to do service work, particularly to guide souls who have recently departed the physical body, helping them to make their transition to their appropriate place within the astral realm and providing them with places of rest, inner healing (if need be) and guidance.

Eventually, the astral realm becomes strictly a realm of service per se. During the course of one's initiation into ever higher levels of light and love, the purifying and clearing away of psychic and psychologically faulty thinking takes place. This is then superseded by right control of the emotions as one moves on to ever higher spheres. In some cases, the only reason one might find him/herself on the astral realm is to serve those still working within the lessons.

It is interesting to note what appears to be of such great and resplendent beauty (as indeed the astral plane does when compared to the physical) is later seen as a limitation to a soul who is developing self-mastery and the more refined qualities of ascension. As plane after plane is mastered and brought under the control of the higher self and monad, so the very substance composing those planes and bodies is likewise elevated and ascended in this process. Eventually, certain bodies (such as the physical/etheric and astral, which we have just discussed) exist merely as points of contact upon that particular plane in order to facilitate service work. Each goal is replaced by a higher goal in an ever-ascending process. Therefore this eventually happens on the astral plane in the same manner that it happens on the Earth plane. The individual soul has purified and heightened the vibrational frequencies to such a high extent that the soul no longer needs that world in order to evolve, but functions there strictly out of desire to serve.

The Mental Realm

There are many similarities between the higher astral realms and the mental realm. Both planes contain varying frequencies, so that souls at various degrees of development can work their way up through the sub-planes of these realms, until, as the lessons are learned and the mastery of certain levels is completed, they find themselves upon the higher levels of that plane. This is not a process unfamiliar to us upon the Earth. For example, a student begins his/her schooling in the lower grades, works through junior high and high school, then works through college and eventually ends up in a master's or Ph.D. program and so forth.

On the mental planes, Cayce's saying that "thoughts are things" could not be more accurate, for the substance of those realms is composed of very refined thought substance and is extremely pliable and reactive to the intent with which we fashion it. The matter of the mental realm responds directly to our thoughts. This is quite a different process than slowly building and bringing forth into manifestation upon the physical that which is first conceived by mind. However, all things begin with the idea and, in this regard, the mental plane is but a reflection of what takes place upon the Earth, albeit at such an accelerated speed as to be nearly instantaneous.

It is on these planes that the ideas of the great souls, great thinkers and masters formulate ideas and work to bring them forth to those who are receptive to them upon the Earth. When there is a new invention, the idea for it has not sprung out of thin air but has been transmitted by thought and inspiration to those who are most receptive.

In this manner does the divine, evolved master scientist work with the mind and brain of the scientist upon Earth. This is so because they who are scientifically inclined, who have their brain cells in a state of readiness to receive additional information, whose minds or "personal data banks" are filled with enough information to utilize the imparted wisdom, are obviously the most suited to receive it. Therefore does the inner-plane scientist work with one so prepared, rather than choose one who is a blank slate in this specialized area.

This holds true for every aspect with which humanity is working. The divine artists, those masters who are developed along these lines and wish to impart the next vision to humanity, will use an artist who works in the particular medium that their vision requires (poetry, literature, painting, music, theater, dance). In this way the vision is most easily brought through and brought into manifestation upon the Earth. To try to inspire a chemist with the next phase of dance would be a fruitless endeavor, as there would be naught within their brain cells with which to either resonate or respond. Whereas, by contacting a receptive dancer or choreographer, there is everything with which to respond, both in the understanding of the idea and in the ability with which to facilitate it and bring it forth into manifestation. Thus, one can see how the creative process is actually a collaboration between certain initiates and masters who work from the mental spheres and those souls who are in physical incarnation.

What I am told by the masters is that the very same soul, when it is advanced enough, can be working simultaneously on the inner mental realms during its hours of sleep and in the physical realms during its waking hours to bring forth the next phase of a project into manifestation. If the soul is very devoted to this project, it might find itself working with the masters on it between incarnations. Then it reincarnates in order to continue that same project and see it through to its full completion. Usually this is done by a chain of initiates who pick up the mantle of responsibility with regard to a certain project. But cases do occur where a particular soul is allowed to bring a specific project to its point of completion.

The Buddhic Realm

The plane next above the mental realm is the buddhic plane, also known in occult literature as the causal plane. This is the realm where the higher self or oversoul has its true habitat. When the individual soul withdraws into that sphere it is able to exist as pure consciousness and pure awareness. One reason the term "causal world" is used to describe this plane is because it is indeed the realm of causation. From this plane the soul can see the causes that it has set in motion and the steps that need to be taken in order to clear away any negative karma that is holding back its evolution or ascension process. The soul can also look at the world of causes for humanity as a whole and see where it can be of greatest service. As we are all connected one to the other, one comes to realize that the best way to advance one's own ascension, liberation or evolutionary process is to help humanity with an attitude of serving the one. From this most glorious realm a soul can see that all are indeed interrelated and that there is no way one can advance by being selfish. One learns on the buddhic plane that to serve the whole is to serve the self and to advance the self is to help the advancement and ascension of the whole. It is this knowledge that will propel humanity forward along the path of ascension.

After death those who have lived a life of service to God and humanity, who are loving and devoted beings, will quickly pass through the etheric, astral and mental realms and take their place in the realm of the higher self. There they will know the "peace that passeth understanding," the bliss that is heretofore unimaginable—utter joy, utter love and utter compassion. There is naught that can exist there but that which holds these qualities divine. For all that the initiate has garnered in the four lower worlds that is of a good, beautiful and true nature will accompany him/her there and all else will be left at the gates of this resplendent realm. When one is liberated from the rounds of birth and death in the lower worlds, the essence of that soul will be taken up with her into this glorious realm, and that essence will contain only the most divine qualities. All lesser qualities will have been karmically worked through and brought to a point of balance where they are no longer active within the initiate's life. That life, henceforth, will be the higher life, and the soul will function as the higher self, who but seeks to serve humanity.

The Atmic Plane

Once connected with the higher self to the aforementioned degree, the soul moves upward to the atmic sphere, where even the limitations of the soul-body are broken through and the connection is then with the monadic self, or the mighty I Am Presence. The soul who has worked its way through the four lower bodies and worlds back to its own realm and thus to a direct connection with its essential self (monad), is now in a place of perfect unity. The soul yet retains its individuality, existing but one realm lower than the monadic plane itself. In the atmic plane the soul is linked to the monad, which is in turn linked with its monadic-group family, working under the influence of the monad, until it works its way back to the monadic plane. There it joins its monadic family, to work from a place of total oneness and beingness.

It is hard to imagine a place of complete and total beingness, yet that is the monadic life. It is a place where naught but unity is known, yet without the loss of individuality. Understand that one functioning from that sphere is functioning in a type of group consciousness that cannot be explained, but will indeed be experienced by all as we make our way back to the monadic source.

The nature of creation is therein revealed as are the answers to all questions. There is total freedom and total bliss. It might surprise some readers to know that a greater evolution awaits the soul itself, one that will take it even beyond the last realm that we shall take under consideration in this book. However, please know that in this place there is no urgency, no worry, no restless uneasiness, but only a state of beingness that knows there are yet vaster realms of beingness to explore.

The Logoic Plane

The last realm that I shall discuss in this book is the logoic plane, which is actually the full realization of the monad or mighty I Am Presence. Because the nature of the cosmos is so vast, I would recommend that for a deeper explanation and exploration of the cosmic planes you refer to my book, *The Complete Ascension Manual*. However, the process of ascension for humanity through the seven planes of existence as it most directly affects us and our individual ascensions is explained thoroughly in this book.

The logoic plane is the plane of total oneness—the I Am Presence. When discussing limitlessness, words can be limiting. Yet, since words are the stairway we climb to further our understanding, they shall have to suffice.

Upon the logoic plane we are put in touch with the intent of God and are at complete oneness with that divine intent and purpose. We know ourselves to be the I Am that I Am and have totally and completely transcended form. We have become that which we sought and are love/wisdom itself. Our will has become the will-to-good which is the will of God. We are completely merged within the whole of things, yet likewise and forever do we retain our individuality. Here have we ascended past our wildest imaginings, for even the soul itself has merged into its planetary source. We henceforth live in complete unity with God, and our will and purpose becomes completely aligned with the will and purpose of the whole. Yet ever the divine paradox holds sway—while merging fully with the one, yet we remain.

Conclusion

We are spiritual beings living in and passing through a variety of spiritual realms. Moreover, we are immortal children of God, and a divine and glorious destiny awaits us all. The process of ascension lies in the experiencing, purifying and mastering of all the realms. Various limitations are experienced as each subsequent realm is mastered. Within each realm we evolve as well, and therefore the energies of the bodies within that realm grow more refined, vibrating at higher frequencies, and thus ascending. There is in reality no death, but only the passing into higher spheres of learning, then returning to the lower or denser ones until the lessons are learned and mastered.

I have presented a brief outline of our spiritual selves and the evolution of them/us through the planes of our relative sphere of divine limitlessness. There is, in truth, evolution that takes place beyond these spheres. But that is the evolution of the soul after it has passed through the processes of initiation and the soul has fully and completely ascended back to its monadic source. I have written about this subject in greater detail in other books and it is not my purpose to go into it here. In this book, I am dealing exclusively with the process of ascension as it concerns us.

2

The Spiritual Hierarchy

The Masters of the Hierarchy

For people new to the path of ascension, I cannot help but feel the confusion one might experience when he/she hears words like "hierarchy" and "ascended beings" thrown about in seemingly casual conversation. I can imagine the frustration one must feel when he/she asks for friendly guidance and is told to call on this or that "master," who holds this or that position in "the Hierarchy." Some of the names of these great beneficent beings sound as though they come from the latest science fiction novel. I am sure that asking for the aid of a being whose name would not be out of place in the same galactic quadrant as *Star Trek*'s Spock, leaves one in a state of utter and understandable bewilderment. The purpose of this book is to eliminate that bewilderment and bring the glory of the Spiritual Hierarchy of masters into reality as fact. I only ask that the reader continues reading with both an open mind and an open heart so that his/her intuition can fully reveal what explanation can only open the doorway to.

A simple analogy is that of the student who begins school at kindergarten age, learns the lessons of the following grades, moves through college, attains a master's degree and then returns to the grade school where he/she first learned the basics and there takes on the role of teacher. This is pretty much the case with those who form the Hierarchy, and even more so with those great beings (whom you might know as world teachers of religions). These teachers come back to the school of Earth to impart to spiritually younger souls the wisdom they garnered moving through the levels of being—a process some of us are only now beginning.

There are, of course, many notable sages, prophets, saints and highly evolved beings who have walked the Earth in flesh and blood. The examples that first come to mind are the Christ (often referred to in occult literature as Lord Maitreya), the Buddha, the Virgin Mary, Moses, Quan Yin and Isis. Also there are the great yogis, mystics and occultists of more modern times such as Yogananda, who founded the Self-Realization Fellowship; Sai Baba, presently the most spiritually advanced being on our planet; Madam Blavatsky and C.W. Leadbeater, who brought through some of the most advanced occult writings in recent history; as well as Alice A. Bailey, who channeled via telepathic link the occult information given by the master Djwhal Khul. I must mention the great spiritual leaders such as Gandhi and Martin Luther King, who guided entire nations toward peace and universal brotherhood, often paying for their commitment with their lives. Even Abraham Lincoln, who, while not in the strictest sense a spiritual leader, was a highly evolved being who led a nation toward peace and paid the ultimate price for his unwavering courage.

When I say that certain souls channel or bring through information given through the telepathic link between them and one of the masters, I mean that these advanced souls who have completed their rounds of birth and death remain on the inner planes and from that abode transmit to the mind of a soul on Earth the guidance they seek to impart to aid humanity's development. Some people with whom they work are themselves masters who have volunteered to come back to serve. Their particular form of service lies in their ability to receive impressions of the master who remains on another plane and thus has a clearer vision of the true nature of reality or who has access to greater vistas of wisdom and love.

Often a disembodied master will work with a disciple or initiate who is consciously working to master his/her lower four bodies to bring them under the influence of the higher aspects of self. These people are on the path of ascension, using all the experiences in their lives to grow and deepen their connection with their higher selves and mighty I Am Presences, or monads. The masters, who have followed the path of ascension, ultimately knowing themselves to be the higher self, come from all religions and all spiritual paths and together form the Hierarchy.

It might be helpful to mention that although these masters are liberated from the physical, etheric, astral and mental worlds, they may choose to incarnate upon any of these planes in order to best carry out their mode of service. Just as Christ, Moses or Buddha incarnated on the Earth, likewise do a host of masters incarnate on the etheric, astral and mental realms to work and serve souls on those realms.

It is important also to realize the planet as a whole is in a state of evolution or process of ascension, so master teachers of one time period have themselves evolved since then and the entire process of ascension itself has been itself speeded up over relatively recent history. Thus humanity is reaching heights en masse that were hitherto reached only by the few.

For the Hierarchy of masters to work to their fullest potential, they seek to be brought forth from behind the shrouds of mystery where they functioned in the past. There are certain fundamentals one needs to understand, so that he/she too can work with them, serve the divine plan and help facilitate his/her own ascension process.

The Hierarchy functions as the Spiritual Government. It is *not* a government like those in any country on Earth; it holds to the highest ideals that inspire all forms of government. They function in a hierarchical structure, and those with lesser vision will happily seek out the greater vision from those beings who possess it. But there is no competition whatsoever, only a joint purpose in serving the whole from places of ever-expanding unity and oneness with the whole. Free and liberated from the pull and dictates of the lower four realms, these beings form a divine structure, each contributing what they are most suited to contribute, each working in their chosen field and appropriate place, yet from a state of utter beatitude, bliss, joy, love and wisdom—a state that we, in our most graced moments, know but as a shadow of the reality in which they live.

Dear readers, the process of ascension has been so accelerated at this time that many who are reading this material are already high-level initiates and disciples who are only hampered by their unfamiliarity with spiritual terminology and process—something that, in truth, they are quite familiar with upon the inner planes. Therefore, for many readers, this book will primarily serve to bring them up to speed with their own evolution and to open a doorway of wisdom that will reveal more about themselves.

The masters themselves have, as a whole, drawn nearer to our world than ever before. This is so because a great many of us are completing our various initiations during this very lifetime, taking the path of ascension and therefore joining the ranks of the masters ourselves. That we all have much to learn is true, but as so many of us are evolving at speeds never before seen upon this planet, the advanced masters are bringing us into ever-greater attunement with their purpose, so that we might learn the needed lessons from them.

Younger Masters

It becomes vital to recognize that many souls have now joined the ranks of the masters of the Spiritual Hierarchy. A group has moved from the fourth, or strictly human kingdom, into the fifth, or spiritual kingdom. There are indeed masters among us. Some who have held their mastership over a vast span of time are more adept at teleportation, bilocation, levitation, healing miracles and so forth. Others of us are masters, but new to that status, so work under the tutelage of a more advanced master, who might be either physically incarnated or not. Some masters remain on other planes, but have the ability to draw the necessary atoms to form a physical, etheric, astral or mental image of themselves with which to communicate with their students.

An example of this type of master can be found among the following, some of whose names might at first sound strange to you, but if meditated upon will have the ring of familiarity to them: Saint Germain, Kuthumi (pronounced Koo-too-mee), Djwhal Khul (pronounced Dwall Cool, sometimes simply referred to as D.K.), Archangel Michael, the Virgin Mary and Jesus. The highest master in physical incarnation, Sai Baba, who lives in a small village in India, may be seen in either the physical/etheric, astral or mental bodies. An incarnated being with his degree of mastership knows no bounds even while in the physical. Born awakened to his God-self, Sai Baba is aptly called an avatar, or a God-realized being from birth.

The newly liberated master has passed either the sixth or the sixth and seventh initiation and has thus achieved the goal of all his lifetimes in this very lifetime. These are the younger masters, sometimes called kindergarten masters, particularly where they have achieved the sixth level of initiation but have to complete the seventh level before becoming a full master. Those in this category are watched over carefully by more advanced masters and worked with daily that we may continue to expand our love, light, power and psychological clarity for the good of all humankind and the Earth as a whole.

I shall delve more deeply into the process of initiation itself in a chapter devoted exclusively to it. But suffice it to say, for the time being, that many reading this may be well on the road to mastery, but simply unfamiliar with the terminology used to express the process they are undergoing. Some very highly developed souls are being born into the world at this time and some of them need just a small degree of openness to be drawn to the place where the teachings of the masters are brought into their conscious minds. It is said that "when the student is ready, the master appears." However, what that statement does not include is the fact that sometimes the student doesn't even know he/she is awaiting the master, except through a dull persistent feeling inside that there is something *more* to life. Well, beloved readers, there is indeed much more to life and the more has come knocking at your door by virtue of your own willingness to explore this seemingly new territory of spiritual and occult understanding.

Bear in mind that there are new members passing through the portals of the sixth and seventh initiation daily. In fact from the time frame of 1995 through the first several years of the next millennium, there will be several waves of mass ascension in which much of humanity will have the window of opportunity to achieve its liberation. As Jesus Christ said, "If you do not believe in me, then believe in the works I do". So I say to you in regard to these souls who are ascending in this lifetime, know them, know each other, know us, by the works we do and not by any outer claim. All who are members of the hierarchy of masters are here to serve. By service we will achieve this great privilege and through service acts we will know each other for who we are.

The Form of the Hierarchy

Here is a brief description of the hierarchical structure. At the head of our solar system, which includes the seven planes discussed earlier, is the cosmic being who holds the position of Solar Logos. He is often referred to as Helios, sometimes jointly as Helios and Vesta. At the head of our planetary system is the Planetary Logos. Until very recently, this high office was held by a being known as Sanat Kumara. The position has now been taken over by he who was, and remains, the Buddha.

Underneath them are three major department heads: The Manu (Allah Gobi), the Mahachohan and the Christ. The position of Planetary Christ is held by Lord Maitreya, who was also Krishna in a previous incarnation.

Below them, and yet still at vast heights, are the masters, or chohans, of the seven rays. There are seven energy types, or rays, expressing themselves in our solar system and planet. The second ray, that of love/wisdom, is the ray or basic energy of the solar system itself. The following is a list of the rays and the masters, or chohans, that head them:

RAY	CHOHAN	ENERGY
First ray	El Morya	Power/will
Second ray	Kuthumi	Love/wisdom
	(Master Djwhal Khul has taken over much of his work, as Kuthumi is preparing to take over the office of the Christ)	
Third ray	Serapis Bey	Active intelligence
Fourth ray	St. Paul the Venetian	Harmony through conflict
Fifth ray	Hilarion	Science and the concrete mind
Sixth ray	Jesus	Devotion
	(Jesus is known on inner planes as Sananda; he was the being whom Christ/Lord Maitreya overlighted 2000 years ago)	
Seventh ray	St. Germain	Ceremonial magic and ritual

Alongside of these work other masters whose areas of expertise are somewhat different. Also, working in graded ranks according to their development are many highly evolved devas, beings whose path of evolution is on the angelic line. From this entire host of divine beings are we offered assistance in our growth process and in every aspect of our lives. There are even groups of masters who are skilled in the art of healing by working with streams of energy. These beings, as well as all the masters and angels, but await our call in order to be of service to us.

It is important to understand that these masters have their own lives on the divine plane of beingness, their own areas of pursuit and their own growth objectives. However, part of what they do is to be actively involved in the evolution of humanity, as well as the Earth as a whole. Some might be more aligned to working with the animal kingdom, while others work specifically with the arts or healing sciences. The point is that no matter what our needs, this hierarchy of beings awaits our call to come forth in loving service to help us in all ways possible. They are here to assist our growth and evolution, and I cannot stress strongly enough the great benefits that are here for us to receive just for the asking. The one thing that they cannot do is infringe upon our free will. And this is why they must be called into action, invited to help us.

If you are doubtful of this, why not begin by calling upon a master with whom you are familiar, such as beloved Jesus, Mother Mary, Moses or the Buddha. See what grace begins to fill you immediately. You might want to experiment by meditating for a brief time on the energy of the specific master you invoked, for example, letting the love and devotion of Jesus fill you or allowing the peace of the Buddha to flow through you. With time, you will come to know the specific masters and their energies quite intimately, and their names will roll off your tongues like a once-familiar language you thought you had forgotten. About these most beloved beings I cannot say anything to better express my personal experience with them than to quote ". . . Prove me now, herewith, sayeth the Lord . . . I shall fill you with blessings that there shall not be room enough to receive them."

3

The Path of Initiation
Ascension and Initiation

The processes of ascension and initiation are inextricably woven together. In order to fully understand the meaning of ascension we must
first understand the process of initiation.

First, here is the broader perspective of what occurs in the life of the
individualized soul as it journeys through the four lower worlds and upward into the spiritual worlds, where self-realization occurs.

When the soul begins its reincarnation process, it is very young from
the point of view of the higher self, or oversoul. The habitat of the higher
self is on the buddhic, or fourth, realm, and during the earlier phases of
the reincarnating soul's experience, the higher self remains detached from
the rudimentary process of the baby soul, which is just beginning to gain
experience in the physical worlds. The soul at this early stage is hardly out
of the animal or instinctive phases of its development. Through the rounds
of birth and death, the soul gradually develops awareness, a just appreciation of right from wrong, and its contact with the physical world becomes
more integrated with its slowly developing astral, emotional and mental
nature.

During these early stages, the emotional, or astral, body is itself
hardly developed. It reacts, rather than acts, and the emotions are of a basic and extreme nature. Seen clairvoyantly, they would appear as flashes
of jagged red, denoting anger or passion, and/or murky brown-grays and
other murky colors that denote vagueness of feeling while simultaneously
revealing greed, lust and the basic instinct of survival. Over time through
incarnation and reincarnation, the astral/feeling body will grow more refined, and the appreciation for beauty, love (beginning first with family,
then community, country and finally life itself), will color the astral aura.

Likewise, at the beginning phases of a soul's process of incarnation

the mental body is barely active. Man's initial ability to think is not far removed from that of an animal's. True, at this point there is some reasoning
ability. However, it is at the most basic level. All thoughts are directed to
the one primal thought—how to survive—and it is around this central
thought that the mind gradually builds its reasoning ability. Slowly, the
young soul figures out how to build shelter, acquire food and protect home.
From this inauspicious beginning the mind gradually learns how to think.
Eventually the thinking process evolves into what is today considered the
norm for most of humanity.

During this slow process of development, the higher self or oversoul,
and to a greater degree the monad, or mighty I Am Presence, is engaged in
the abstract lives of the higher realms, allowing that part of itself which is
developing through the rounds of birth and death to find its own way. It is
only when the soul reaches a certain degree of development that the higher
self and monad begin to take an active interest in that soul. It is also during these later stages that the reincarnating soul turns toward its higher
self and, through the sensing of the higher presence, begins to pray and
ask assistance from this higher aspect of self. It is then that the soul, taking responsibility for its evolution, truly begins to join in purpose with the
higher self. The soul is then considered to be officially on the probationary
path. And thus the stage is set for the soul to tread the path of discipleship
and initiation.

The Probationary Path

The soul upon the probationary path now turns its attention to the
world and influence of the higher self, or oversoul. In turn, the higher self
vaguely begins to turn its attention to that part of itself going through the
rounds of incarnation within the four lower worlds. Although not yet officially on the path of initiation, it is at the very beginning of that path. And
hence the soul, or person, also attracts the attention of the master and
group of masters to which it is linked by certain cosmic laws of attraction.
The point is that the soul/person is now under the watchful eye of both the
master and the higher self, and henceforth continues the process of reincarnation under the guiding forces of the divine.

It must be noted that, at this early stage known as probation, the person is generally not aware of this connection at all. This period is about the
giving by the master to the probationer a greater stimulation of light and
divine impressions, which again, the person is not awake to. It is the waiting to see period—to see what the person will do with such stimulation.

As the probationer works unconscious of his/her connection to the
higher self and master, it remains up to him to choose from his own re-
sources just how he will respond. This period is then governed by the

person's own choices as to what he does with the influx of divine stimulation and at what rate of speed he will evolve. Progress is determined by the development of the higher principles as they become more active in the probationer's life. A master can see this through the auric emanations of that person.

The Accepted Disciple

This phase of initiation on the path of ascension marks the real beginning of the work between disciple and master. Now, the master has blended, albeit loosely, his own aura with that of the disciple. This blend allows the master to work more directly with the disciple in a variety of ways, yet it is relegated to the periphery of the master's aura because the new disciple still tends to experience emotions that the master wants kept at bay. But the link and blend are established enough that the disciple's initiation/ascension process may begin to receive some very direct attention, and the master will be protected from the disciple's still-rapidly fluctuating mood swings and disturbing thought tendencies.

The incarnated soul must now establish him/herself in the world of service. The person must begin to manifest, within his sphere of influence, the qualities of love, light, compassion and divine intent. These qualities will grow and deepen as he proceeds along the path of initiation and ascension. But once a person has become an accepted disciple, attention must be paid to developing these higher qualities.

One technique that quickly effectuates this is meditation. There is a variety of meditations, some more powerful than others and some simply better suited to the needs and temperament of a specific disciple. Regardless of the technique, the goal must be the same: focusing on quieting the emotional and mental bodies as well as the physical body. This is so that the higher self may find the person in a receptive state of readiness where it can communicate certain impressions from the higher realm. The master also needs to find the disciple in a quiet and centered state of readiness to impart the higher teachings, stimulations and activations that will develop the soul/person and inspire him/her to greater heights.

I have practiced a variety of meditative techniques at different points along my path. Two favorites are techniques taught by the Self-Realization Fellowship through Yogananda and his lineage of master teachers and those taught by Astara, given by the master Kuthumi through Earlyne and Robert Chaney. Also, I have developed my own meditations and activations, which are contained in my book, *The Complete Ascension Manual*. These meditations deal primarily with quieting the four lower bodies and invoking the masters to help deepen the higher self and monadic connection. Meditation need not be a complicated procedure involving challenging breathing techniques, but can simply be a centering and quieting of the four-body system. At the same time we call forth the higher aspects of self and the masters to quickly and safely infuse the divine qualities within the four lower bodies. In this way we become linked and blended with the higher self, monad and masters in ever-deepening degrees.

Through meditation, service, love, compassion, light and the will-to-good, we advance as disciples. If we continue steadfastly in this manner, before we know it we will be moving through the various initiations consciously working on our paths of ascension. Actually, initiation and ascension are but two sides of the same coin. We go through initiation in a systematic order by sequentially and simultaneously mastering the four bodies, as well as becoming infused with our higher selves and monads to greater and greater degrees. This aligns us with our particular lineage of masters, so that we may expediently find our right work or most harmonious and appropriate path of service. While this is occurring, so is the light and love within us growing, along with the purifying and clearing of our psychic and psychological selves. In this manner we become accepted initiates and begin in earnest to hasten our work upon the path of ascension.

The paths of initiation and ascension are in a real sense one and the same path and process, though often delineated and expressed through different modes of interpretation. For example, an initiate is said to have reached such-and-such a light quotient on his/her path of ascension and therefore is at such-and-such a stage of initiation. What is really happening is that the same thing is being expressed from two different angles or lenses. However, the paths of both initiation and ascension are actually the same. One cannot exist without the other.

It is vital to know that the level of one's initiation does reveal how far one has come along the path of ascension, so he/she may gain greater insight into that stage: (To find out about your level of initiation, call my number [listed in the back of this book] and I will set you up with a channeled reading from the masters.)

The First Initiation

The first initiation is truly the official stepping of the soul onto the path of ascension. What has occurred until one enters the probationary path is now put into full force. The act of gaining self-mastery is now an integral part of the person's very purpose.

The first vehicle of self-mastery is twofold. It involves mastering the basic lower physical tendencies by purifying the diet, keeping the body free from toxins as much as possible and using pure water to cleanse both the inner and outer physical vehicle. This process will continue to be refined throughout subsequent initiations, but a definite stand of physical mastery over the lower aspects and a certain amount of purifying the body will have occurred during the first initiation.

This aspect of physical mastery will coincide with the beginning stages of mastering the astral body. Another name for the first initiation is the birth, the birth of love in its purest form. With this higher love force in operation begins the transmutation of lust into love, as the initiate is now functioning from the heart center. By this overlapping of goals in the first initiation, one can see how the bodies and realms (physical and emotional) are interpenetrating and overlapping.

During this initiation the person-as-the-soul begins to become aware of him/herself as the soul. This is not necessarily brought through to the conscious mind, however. On the inner planes, and during certain periods of meditation, one senses that her life is more than simply the one life she is currently involved in. She senses that she is something more than mere flesh and blood, more than the sum total of this single earthly life—a soul incarnate connected to a vaster purpose.

The Second Initiation

The second initiation deals more fully with the control of the astral/emotional body. During this period the initiate devotes much time and energy to mastering the desire self, so that the higher desires of the soul may supersede the lower, uncontrolled desires of the personality.

The aspirations of the second-degree initiate reach upward to that of the oversoul itself, and he/she becomes inspired. Selfish desires are replaced by the desire to serve; selfish love yields, to a certain degree, to unconditional love. This is the perfect opportunity—one that truly must be taken—to work with the psychological nature of ourselves. This will lead to more in-depth psychological work, which will be further refined during the third, or soul merge, initiation. However, this is the point when emotional and psychological cleansing must begin.

As we deal with mastering the emotional/desire body, this is the perfect place to see just what our motivations, our strengths and weaknesses are in regard to our feeling world. Where do we yield most easily to violent emotions of any nature and how can we transmute those negative tendencies? One surefire answer lies in our willingness to ask it, and therefore bring it out from subconscious domination so we may master it. Since we need psychological clarity and purification to truly and finally complete our ultimate goal of ascension, it is best to begin by checking in with the emotional body and working with any disruption and turbulence that comes to our awareness.

Here again, meditation plays a key role. By stilling the emotional body, by picturing it calm and clear as a pure and peaceful pool of water, unruffled by winds of confusion, we create the space for the emotional self to exist in that manner. By such meditation and visualization we allow the emotions to rest and be in pure and utter quietude. In this way we bring the desire nature into a state of calm and restful repose, which is then carried forward after the period of deep meditation. This requires constant vigilance on our parts, holding the attitude of mastery over the mood swing of desire, which comes and goes in the life of the second-degree initiate. But this is applicable to us all in varying degrees, even during the later stages of our initiation or ascension process. To pass through the portals of the second initiation however, one must begin to effectuate this mastery to a designated degree, and the more work we do in the initial stages, the easier it will be for us later on.

Since in this step each initiate becomes somewhat aware of his/her higher self, he also becomes aware that he is working with a soul family, or soul group, and not functioning only as an individualized soul. This is but the beginning glimpse, however, of what the third initiation will bring about in a more definitive way. There is an expanded feeling of unity and a noble desire to progress—not just for the self alone, but for the greater whole to which one now senses he belongs.

The ultimate goal of the second initiation is to merge one's personal goals and desires with that of the whole, of which the initiate now feels himself a part. But in order to truly accomplish this, the initiate must work diligently to clear away all debris that has served as personal emotional blocks to this process. This is accomplished by practicing unconditional love and service and daily attitudinal healing (thoughts cause our feelings) and focusing on quieting the emotional body. Finally, this is done by a willingness to proceed with the necessary psychological work required to clear the emotional body of false beliefs.

The many psychological-healing aids to work with include: affirmations, journal-writing, positive visualizations and communicating with the inner child. Those are but a few examples I draw your attention to so that you may begin working immediately in this area. I would recommend also reading my book *Soul Psychology* to accelerate this process. I stress this so emphatically because often one meets but the bare requirements of this initiation and proceeds forward, only to be continually confronted with these same issues as he/she moves up the ascension ladder.

It is said that a word to the wise is sufficient. Let the word then go forth that self-mastery over the desires and emotional nature cannot be taken seriously enough. To proceed through the higher initiations in as safe and swift a manner as possible, do not be content simply to fulfill the minimum requirements of control over the emotional body. Save yourself the trouble of having to learn the deeper lessons later on by implementing as complete a program as possible now, thus clearing and healing any sore points within that aspect of self during this second level on your pathway of ascension. The beginning stages of inner peace are a signpost that you are achieving this goal. However, do not be afraid of feelings of unsettlement that go along with the transmutation from negative ego to spiritualized ego, for there is much adjustment required. Trust me, any discomfort you might at first feel is well worth it, as the ultimate benefits you will receive are manna from heaven.

The Third Initiation

Another name for the third initiation is the soul merge, because it is through this initiation that one becomes directly linked with the higher self, or oversoul. Both the higher self and the masters begin to work directly with the soul in incarnation, or you, the person now reading this book. The relationship between this higher aspect of self and the masters is now brought into full play, and the merger between the person and the oversoul is put into complete effect. Because the initiate is now merged with the oversoul, he/she now becomes aware that she belongs to a soul family and through meditation can intuit this fact. Therefore the work of this initiate becomes more geared to group purpose than ever before.

At this initiation mastery over thought must be a central focus. Thought forms must become clear and well defined and their purpose must be twofold. First, they must be aimed at the control of the mental world and mental body of the initiate, and this will deepen the process of self-purification. Second, thoughts must be aimed at fulfilling the plan as it affects group service, both of the immediate soul family and of the entire world family of which the soul, soul family and monad, or mighty I Am Presence, are all a part. I include the monad at this point, for it is at this initiation that the monad begins to have a direct impact upon the oversoul, and therefore, the soul in incarnation.

Bear in mind that we are now talking about those who have merged with their oversouls and are soul-infused personalities. And yet there remains much work to be done. Nevertheless, they have made definite progress upon their path of ascension and show signs of those who have taken the soul merge—unconditional love and a passionate desire to serve humanity.

The majority of work during the third initiation focuses primarily on thought control. At this stage initiates must learn to master their own thought worlds, rather than be victims of habitual thought or the thought forms of mass consciousness. To be honest, full mastery of this realm will extend over subsequent initiations, but a certain degree of mastery must be attained to move forward through the third initiation. It is one of the most important lessons one can learn. As Sai Baba said in *Voice of the Avatar* ". . . the mind is said to be the instrument for both bondage and liberation."

Most of us do not realize how hypnotized we are by the world's point of view. We accept things as fact simply because the news magazines, teachers and others portray them as such. This is not truth as God would have us see it, but rather as the forces of business, politics, media and the joint thought form of the earthly controlling powers would have us believe.

Our own consciousnesses are filled with certain detrimental thought processes that were passed along to us since we first made our entrance into this world. They have been filtered into our consciousness through outside influences, but also from our parents, who were themselves victims of mass thought. Then these thoughts were further shaped and molded by experiences in the world—all serving to validate this faulty thinking. That is why I have offered throughout my books various techniques to reprogram the thought process in a more positive, spiritual and healthy manner.

The most important thing one can do is set the intent to work within the spheres of thought in the most productive way possible. The entirety of one's thought world is not expected to reach ultimate mastery during this initiation. However, the intent to create the clearest, healthiest and most spiritual thoughts must, by this stage, be firmly set in motion. And along with this intent must come action—thought action, which I shall illustrate with the following example.

Suppose you are driving and someone cuts you off. The immediate thought response of most people would be some type of expletive and/or gesture of a lower nature. What happens with thoughts of this nature is that they do indeed take shape, color and form. These thoughts are then sent to the person who has cut you off. And, quick as a thought, you have put him/her under psychic attack!

This is one small example of how most people go about each day, unaware of the negative thoughts they are unconsciously throwing out into the world. And if the person in the offending car is of a sensitive nature, he/she will psychically pick up your thought, and, depending upon his particular nature, will either feel hurt by it or react with a strong negative thought thrown back at you! This type of thinking serves only to fill our atmosphere with psychic debris that we could do very well without. Who knows, that person who cut you off might be rushing home to a dire family crisis and in need of spiritual, loving, supportive thoughts. Whatever the situation, why not work as an initiate (as do the masters) and bless the world rather than curse it.

There is a simple technique that many people, including myself, use to defuse the flow of negative thoughts. I call it the bless-instead-of-curse technique. Whenever you find yourself in a situation like the one above and your first impulse is to think or say, "Oh negative word, negative word, negative word," turn it quickly around and instead think or say, "Oh, bless you." This might feel a bit unfamiliar and strange at first, but I assure you, it works wonders. Even in the case of a stubbed toe, when you want to think, shout or mutter colorful expletives, try something like "thank you for this lesson, thank you for this lesson, thank you for this lesson," until the pain subsides. This might sound a bit funny, but it tremendously changes the mental atmosphere around you.

This type of thinking also works as a shield of protection against other people's negative thought forms. When you align yourself with the light and love and positivity that is available, other people's negative energy will roll off you like water off a duck's back. By putting this into daily practice you will truly be working on the side of the masters, cleansing and purifying the mental world in which we live. You will likewise grow more adept at controlling your own thoughts and thus find yourself helping raise the vibration of the planet by making these simple changes in thought habits.

However, be sure that you do not fall into the trap of thought repression. This process of initiation is one of growth and transcendence, not one of repression. So use the tools I have suggested, or any others that you feel are helpful, to cleanse your thought world by healing, not repressing. Journal-writing to see what is going on in the depths of your inner self is also a wonderful idea. At some point, you might want to seek a combination of spiritual and psychological counseling.

Everything on the spiritual path should have a balance to it; or as the Buddha said, "Walk the middle road." Do the work, but do it honestly without stuffing anything down. Work through blockages in the mental as well as the emotional body and world, rather than trying to avoid or deny them. In this manner, both you and the planet as a whole will ascend into the love and light of your true beingness—quickly, safely and purely.

Understand that there are two forms of denial. Healthy denial is the positive process of not allowing negative, egocentric thoughts to enter your conscious mind. Unhealthy denial is to deny reality or deny the truth of what is really going on within self. This could also take the form of denying positive or spiritual thoughts. For example, you might get into an argument with your spouse and the thought to apologize or maybe forgive enters your mind. The negative-ego aspect within your mind tells you to hold onto anger and false pride. In this example, you might deny the impulse and thought instead of following the higher self's guidance. To deny the urge to hold onto anger and false pride would be the healthy form of denial. In an example of unhealthy denial, a person is told by a friend that he is being too egotistical. The person might deny the truth of this feedback to both his friend and to himself, but on a subconscious level, this is exactly what is going on. Hence, we arrive at the adage, "Know thyself." It is up to you to keep careful watch to develop a true perception of reality toward self and others. We don't just see with our eyes but also with our minds and belief systems. Thoughts create our reality. This is why it is so important to develop mastery over the mind in the third initiation and beyond.

In traditional psychology, repression is the negative use of denial. Suppression is the healthy use of denial. Therefore, bear in mind that to keep negative egotistical thinking from entering your conscious mind by consciously denying opportunity is essential to developing inner peace. Likewise, repeating positive thoughts, affirmations and visualizations is essential in reprogramming both the conscious and subconscious minds to develop a habit of thinking properly, which then leads to positive feelings, emotions, actions and manifestation.

The Fourth Initiation

The fourth initiation has been called the crucifixion. This is because all outer props, dependencies and supports have been taken away or fail to give the familiar satisfaction they did before this particular initiation. One is then left to rely solely upon his/her relationship to self, God and the masters. There is a period of sacrifice and letting go that accompanies this initiation. Any aspect of fear or loss that one feels during this period lasts only until the initiate learns to look at life truly as a series of lessons and to view everything through the lens of the higher self and monad. What might be perceived as loss is really only the negative-ego aspect of self holding onto things that the spiritual mind recognizes the initiate doesn't really want or need. So, in truth, nothing is lost except lower-self desire, which is transformed into higher-self desire.

On the higher level—specifically the buddhic realm, or causal or fourth realm—the body or form that inhibited the soul from its full and complete expression is burned up, so to speak. In this way the inner plane corresponds to the outer plane period called the crucifixion. In essence, the part of oneself that nurtured the growth of the soul on the physical, etheric, astral and mental realms and held all the spiritual expressions and experiences of that self is, on a symbolic level, an egg. In fact, the shape of the causal or buddhic vehicle is often compared to an egg, so I merely continue the analogy.

At the fourth initiation, all of the good, the beautiful and the true that is contained within the egg seeks even greater expression. On its own buddhic plane, the oversoul breaks through the shell that contained it, much like a chick breaks out of its shell at the time of hatching. At this point the initiate has merged with the soul, and the soul body is no longer needed. The initiate becomes the oversoul/higher self, or an extension of the monad. They then communicate through what is called the *antakarana*, or rainbow bridge. In essence, the initiate has a change of teachers. The monad/spirit/mighty I Am Presence becomes the new teacher, replacing the higher self, which has now fully merged with the initiate.

The subtleties at this level are a bit harder to translate into language than at the level of the four lower bodies. But, suffice it to say, it is at this initiation that one becomes a soul unencumbered, now able to make direct contact with the monad itself, without the soul body which served as an intermediary before this phase. The process of ascension, initiation, learning and growth is not yet complete. When seen through the higher lens of the monad, it is a process that is infinite. However, the major initiations that are to be dealt with in this book are one through seven, with the fourth being one of extreme significance. In essence, it is merely the soul encasement that is burned up. And all the virtue gained from past lives inside the egg, or encasement, is now mystically raised into the monad. This adds a brilliance to the true home of one's being. One is now being spirit rather than oversoul—oversoul having been the intermediate teacher throughout the ages until the initiate could realize this initiation.

At this point, vision has grown by leaps and bounds and the interest is truly in elevating the world, since the soul knows itself to be one with All That Is. All efforts are now bent toward working off the last vestiges of personal karma, while at the same time seeing clearly enough to focus on aiding the world through the balancing and adjusting of karma for the planet as a whole.

The initiate is no longer considered the soul in prison but the soul itself. The fourth-level initiate sees the world from the vantage point of soul, which is from above downward. The connection with the higher self is there for the asking, since he/she knows herself to be that higher self, now seeking guidance from the monadic level. Although known as the initiation of crucifixion, it is ultimately the initiation of *freedom*. The fourth-degree initiate is now the soul seeking greater communion with spirit/monad, or the mighty I Am Presence.

The Fifth Initiation

The fifth initiation is known as the monadic merger. The third initiation was known as the soul merge, for the soul incarnate began to fully identify itself with the oversoul. Now at this higher phase the spiritual initiate, who knows himself to be the higher self, begins the process of merging with the monad or mighty I Am Presence itself on Earth. Another name for this initiation is the revelation and it occurs on the atmic, or fifth, plane.

At this point the relationship is between the individualized spiritual person/soul and the monad. The impressions received come forth directly from the monadic plane and the masters. The will to serve becomes of paramount importance, as the vision of the fifth-degree initiate includes both the many levels of the human kingdom and the spiritual kingdom. As the greater vision always includes the lesser, likewise the initiate becomes aware of the animal, vegetable and mineral kingdoms' roles in the evolution of Earth, as well as that of the angelic line.

What might be of esoteric interest here is that the hierarchy is sometimes called the Great White Lodge or the Great White Brotherhood. The masters are often referred to in this manner when being discussed as a group. The word "white" in this case has nothing to do with race; rather it stands for that aspect of being that includes all the colors within it and, additionally, for purity. The higher aspect of the Great White Brotherhood is known as the Sirian Brotherhood or Lodge, to which an initiate gains acceptance at the fifth initiation. There a whole new vista of revelations awaits them. To quote a favorite passage from Djwhal Khul's channeling in *The Rays and the Initiations* through Alice Bailey, ". . . each initiation achieved but reveals still higher ones to be mastered, and never comes the point where the aspirant (be he an average man, an initiate, a master, a chohan or a buddha) can remain in a condition static, and is incapable of future progress."

When I first read this it made such an impression that I kept referring to it for meditation. This little passage reveals so much, for it puts into perspective just how vast the process of initiation and ascension is, and it likewise affirms that we, as human beings, souls and monads, have a cosmic destiny within that great vastness of being. So it is for the fifth-degree initiate, who is at the point of being connected with his/her monad and moving into undreamed-of spheres. This, my beloved readers, is our divine destiny—to reach these heights and continue to ascend.

It must be understood that ascension, in truth, is really descension. By this I mean, in the ascension process one is not leaving the Earth, but rather anchoring first the oversoul and then the monad, or mighty I Am Presence, into the four-body system on Earth. So ascension is really the descension of oversoul and spirit into the worlds of matter. In essence then, the ascended being is God made manifest upon Earth. This is God's true divine plan—to create heaven on Earth. And this, my beloved readers, we are all a part.

The Sixth Initiation

The sixth initiation is the initiation of ascension, which is a process that from one angle, begins at the sixth initiation and is concluded at the completion of the seventh initiation. From a broader perspective, the process of ascension begins with the start of the probationary path and continues into vast and almost-unfathomable cosmic realms. However, it is vital to note that at the sixth initiation one is considered a kindergarten ascended master and at the seventh initiation, a full-fledged ascended master.

The sixth initiation occurs on the monadic, or sixth, plane of being itself. This is a momentous occasion—the point at which the initiate and the monad merge directly. One knows as fact that he/she is the I Am that I Am, the mighty I Am Presence, that which we call God, and likewise, that All That Is is God. One sees through a lens of total unity, of complete and utter oneness, therefore experiencing joy, unconditional love divine and the peace that passeth understanding.

A statement by Paramahansa Yogananda, although not specifically addressing the sixth initiation, is quite applicable here. He said, and I paraphrase, that you go along day after day, working on yourself, practicing yoga, studying, meditating and so forth, and then suddenly you find *yourself* being called "master." That is pretty much my feeling about this initiation. You work hard on purifying the four lower bodies, bringing yourself into alignment with your oversoul and monad, and then one day you find that all this has paid off and you have become that which you sought.

There is no way one can reach the sixth initiation without doing the necessary work on every level of one's being. Light must be invoked, and equally, love must be invoked. Light and unconditional love are two interwoven parts of one whole, and the initiate must learn how to embrace, embody and manifest both divine qualities within his/her very being. The more light and love, the higher one goes on the path of ascension. However, in order to be a clear channel and expression of the mighty I Am Presence, one must clear out all of the dross within his lower vehicle. Even after one takes this magnificent initiation, he must keep vigilant watch over these parts of himself, that he remain clear and centered enough to do the service work that his monad inspires him to. That is why I encourage cleansing the psychological self at the earlier stages, so the vessel of our four lower bodies remains in a state of readiness to serve, free from psychic debris of the lower self, and under the mastery of the highest self.

Many initiates would like to bypass working with the four-body system, but ultimately, this cannot be done. There is no way out but through, and if we seek to become full-fledged masters, then the earlier we begin working with our stuff or negative-ego blockages, the easier we will move through the levels into the monadic level of ascension. We will all be the better for it as well, for even a sixth- and seventh-level initiate (when within the four lower worlds) has those bodies to contend with. For those of us already in the habit of clearing the negative ego, our service missions will be that much easier. We will remain connected to the monadic plane, and without hindrance know the totality of joy, peace and unconditional love that such a connection brings.

On the monadic plane, where the initiate is at last one with the One and merged with the whole, he/she retains her individuality. There seems to be a concern whether or not, when merged with the whole, we lose our separate identities. I mentioned this previously but restate it from this realm. All that the individual soul is or has been that comprises the individuality, still remains. The negative ego is released, the lower energies are dissipated, but the spiritual qualities we have cultivated are brought forth with us to enrich the whole.

No one need fear losing him/herself in the process of ascension. On the contrary, what happens is that each person/soul finally finds himself. To again quote Djwhal Khul through Alice Bailey in *Ponder on This* ". . . the initiate is a conscious aspect of that of which he forms an integral part."

This, my beloved readers, is the glory of ascension for the sixth degree initiate. The glory of which I speak finds its culmination in taking and completing the seventh initiation, which we shall now explore.

The Seventh Initiation

The seventh initiation marks full ascension. It takes place upon the logoic, or seventh, plane and is also known as the resurrection. This is the goal for which every initiate strives. It is the full and complete liberation of which the yogis speak. It is the nirvana of the Buddhist. It is the highest stage of *samadhi*, which is the ultimate goal of the meditator. It is being our full and complete essential monadic selves. We are, henceforth, no longer called forth into the lower worlds, other than by our own free choice in a desire to serve or in the pure seeing the need of the hour. Those who so choose to come back are known as *bodhisattvas*, they who remain to serve out of compassion. The seventh-degree initiate is fully ascended and free, functioning on the highest planes in blissful unity with the one.

I earlier mentioned the Great Lodge of Sirius and the vastness of cosmic expansions. Into these realms the seventh-degree initiate ventures forth. The cosmos is vast and holds no limitation, and from the logoic plane these vaster reaches are accessible, as stage by stage even the ascended master continues to evolve. I mention that again here, lest the mind begin to put limits on that which is limitless. The spiritual and cosmic destiny of a fully ascended master is great indeed. In the ultimate sense there are 352 levels of initiation to be mastered to achieve what I call cosmic ascension (as opposed to planetary ascension, which I have been speaking of previously in this book).

What we cannot ignore is that even higher sources than those which we will primarily focus do have an impact on the ascended master. Therefore I ask you to read the following with an open mind and, more importantly, an open heart. It is actually the heart and intuition that convey the higher truth more significantly than does the mind. As it has so often been said, God is love. And it is through the combined energies of that love and light that we will be able to intuit the truths found upon the higher realms.

The spiritual will is fully activated upon the logoic plane. This comes into full functioning, along with unconditional love and wisdom, which are the very qualities of our particular solar system. These divine qualities, along with certain divine attributes that may be brought forth for the specific mission of the ascended master—the power of bilocation, telepathy, the ability to live on pure light, for example—are all aimed toward the purpose of service. (The advanced ascended-master abilities are not realistically available until the integration of the twelfth level, reached after achieving planetary ascension.)

The inner-plane ascended masters are available to each and every one of us to help on our own paths of ascension. Since the various masters have differing areas of expertise, the more we learn about them, the more specific we can be in directing our prayer requests to them. If we but pray to God, however, the masters will hear our prayers and those who are best suited to help with our particular dilemmas will surely respond. Also, the mere act of reading this book automatically connects us with the ascended masters and they eagerly await our slightest requests to help in any way possible.

During sleep and meditation, we who have reached this level of ascension likewise work with those who form our own body of students. This need not be something we bring forth into full waking consciousness, although with time and practice we do grow ever more adept at doing so. Nevertheless this is a service many render, often during sleep time. Therefore, we need not be surprised if a certain person with whom we are working says he/she has seen us appear in his dreams. Some of these students will find us on the physical realms. Others will know us etherically, while still others will be confined to our work on the astral and mental realms, just as we have the masters above us who help us move onward.

The structure of the Hierarchy manifests itself very early on. The first-degree initiate has much to offer the probationer. The second-degree initiate has much to offer the first, the third-degree initiate has much to impart to the second and so on. Therefore the love and wisdom of one level is always available to those who are reaching up from the level below. The one great truth and gift of the hierarchical structure that differentiates it from the masses of men and the more ordinary forms of rank is that within the aura of the hierarchy of initiates and masters, the call for help falls upon ears of loving compassion, and the desire to serve rules therein. It differs from the desire to control or manipulate that is so often found among the masses. If one senses any degree of control or manipulation coming from an elder member of the Hierarchy, then he/she should recognize that that person has temporarily lost his way and the initiate should seek help from purer sources. Unconditional love, purity of motive and the brightness of one's light will shine within the aura of the true master.

Know that the seventh level of initiation is indeed available to all humanity. It is, in truth, the divine destiny of each of us to reach these heights and beyond, regardless of religious affiliation, spiritual path or the diverse possibilities of spiritual teachers with whom an Earth person might be connected. The doorway of opportunity to pass quickly through the various initiations of ascension has never been swung so wide as during this particular time period. The invitation to ascension is being made by God, and it lies within our own wills whether we choose to take advantage of it. There is, however, no judgment as to how slow or fast we desire to move through this process, for eventually we shall all find our way home within the appropriate time frame. This applies to every human being on Earth, whether he/she believes in the concept of initiations and ascension or not.

Most initiations are actually taken on the inner plane at night during sleep, so it is common for disciples and initiates not to be consciously aware of this process. Occasionally this is made known through a dream or meditation experience.) Many advanced initiates do not remember any of this, but it does not change the essential truth of it. All they might need is a simple prod to remember to connect with the reality of their ascension and initiation process. Reading a simple book such as this might, in fact, be all the stimulus they need to rekindle this remembrance.

For those reading this book, I would venture to guess that you would choose now rather than later to embrace your spiritual path—that something within you has drawn you to investigate this subject. I would further guess that it is the call of your higher self, or perhaps even your monad, that has led you to ponder the path of ascension and the nature of your being. Follow that high calling, beloved readers, for it is the call of the highest and best within you. The discovery that the kingdom of heaven lies within is the most glorious, wondrous, spectacular and divine discovery you can ever make. The "many mansions within the Father's house" are too glorious to even attempt to express, and yet I have tried in this chapter to offer you glimpses of them. In truth, all I have explained about the initiations are but tiny candles glowing in the immense expanse of the myriad windows of the Father's mansions. I hope these candles will shed some light to the conscious mind about what is truly known only to those souls who venture forth into their own divinity by actually walking the path.

Finally, you should know that you do not have to change religions, spiritual teachers, or spiritual paths to embrace the ascension process spoken of in this book. All that is required is a willingness to open your mind and heart to these teachings and then simply blend and integrate them into the religion or spiritual path that you are most compatible with and/or feel guided to be upon.

4

The Psychology of Ascension
The Importance of Love

I cannot emphasize strongly enough the importance of the role love plays in the process of ascension. There are many books devoted to the importance of cultivating the inner light, including many of my own, and this is of great significance. What we must not overlook, however, is the true cultivation of unconditional love. I am not talking here about sentimental love, although that has its place in the scheme of things. I am specifically addressing the quality of *divine* love, which permeates every aspect of our beings, and is an intrinsic part of our nature.

All too often people on the path of ascension spend so much time developing the light and wisdom aspects of self that they in essence close down *heart*. Without an open heart you can get just so far. The statement "God is love" is not a sentimental one but a fact. It is one of the essential qualities at the very core of this solar system. The love/heart nature of God and ourselves is in dire need of attention as we seek to follow the path of initiation and ascension.

What must eventually take place within each and every one of us is a complete integration of the four-body system with that of the higher bodies. In this process, none of the divine attributes that comprise ourselves on any level of our beings can be overlooked. The lower-self qualities, or negative-ego qualities, must be brought under the control of the conscious mind and replaced with the higher, christed or spiritual qualities of the oversoul and monad. We must therefore work with that blessed attribute of love. In this process we clear away all hindrances to love's true and full expression by working through the blocks that exist in our subconscious minds. We likewise work with learning how to invoke the quality of divine love, which will descend upon us when called forth sincerely, as a downpouring from the very heart of God itself.

Because many of us were brought up with certain fears, mistrusts, shame and misuse of love, we tend to steer clear of love. This is generally not a conscious decision. It stems from the subconscious mind and the inner child, which has often been wounded at an early age by the misuse of power and manipulation put upon us in the name of love or by the all-too-common conditional love that our parents gave us as infants, children and throughout much of our adult lives. I am not here to judge anyone who has misused love, for this is what the mass of humanity has been taught to do. I am here, however, to reveal areas where this has occurred and to unmask the distortions that have been placed on loving, so that we may first learn how to love by learning to love ourselves. This I will do by both exposing our faulty belief systems and fears and by offering tools to promote the needed healing.

Loving Self

The ability to love begins with the ability to love oneself. Without self-love, it is impossible to truly love another human being. The person who is filled with shame, fear, guilt and low self-esteem will ever be at odds within him/herself and therefore at odds with the world. This most basic issue of self-love must be addressed, since without it true progress upon the path of initiation and ascension will inevitably be disrupted and unbalanced.

Humanity tends to try circumventing certain areas of difficulty by unhealthily repressing feelings, which in truth need to be healed. This is very true in regard to loving. As the negative ego tries to deceive you into falsely believing that you are operating out of a place of love or keeps you in a tape-loop of defensiveness against any real heart connections within yourself and with the world, it is vital that you summon forth the courage to see just what level your self-love is operating from.

If you find you are hiding behind a fortress of repression and are a victim of low self-esteem, then now is the time to face that fact and be utterly honest with yourself.

One of the prime areas where we have been shaped to conditional love is during interactions with our parents, who are to the infant-self the very world itself. They generally exhibit to us a love that is most conditional. If we behave properly, we are rewarded. If, however, we behave in a manner not to their liking the love is seemingly withdrawn. This is usually done with no malicious intent; it is simply the parents acting out what they have learned in relation to teachings they have received from the world.

Every parent, teacher, institution and government needs to be aware of just how damaging this type of behavior is. The fact remains, however, that to effectuate change we must begin with ourselves, and here that means clearing the subconscious mind from faulty belief systems, low self-esteem and the actions and reactions of the negative ego. We must learn how to love ourselves right where we are now, with all our seeming faults, failures and fears. This might take some work, particularly if you have a very low opinion of yourself, but I am here to remind you that you are a divine child of God. Love is your *birthright*. It is who and what you essentially are. Therefore, let us begin to work with some basic tools to change the faulty belief you might have in regard to your self-worth and self-love and replace it by acknowledging now that you are worthy of all the love in the cosmos simply because you *are*.

Reprogramming Self to Self-Love

Let us first realize that none of us are stuck with negative-ego programming. Everyone has the power to change this programming through higher self and conscious mind, and I now ask you to join me in that adventurous journey toward self-love.

Self-Love Meditation

Find a comfortable position, either lying down or sitting up.

Allow the breath to flow easily and naturally.

Feel the support of the earth below and the heavens above.

Relax into the flow of your breathing.

Begin to quietly mouth the words, "I love myself because I am a son/daughter of God, I love myself because I am a son/daughter of God . . . I love myself because I am a son/daughter of God."

If you feel like saying this aloud, then do so.

If you feel like whispering or mouthing the words, then do that.

If you feel like saying this mantra out loud or chanting quietly to yourself, then proceed that way.

Follow the path that feels most appropriate, but give at least three to five minutes of your time to affirm the fact that you do indeed love yourself.

When you feel ready, find at least three aspects of yourself that you feel to be lovable and voice those in a like fashion.

You may simply say, "I love myself because I am lovable."

You might want to say, "I love myself because it feels good to love myself."

The point is that you don't need to find yourself lovable because of any achievements, but rather let your self-love feelings flow simply out of your divine birthright to be loved. Stay with these affirmations for an-

other three-to-five-minute period, or longer if you desire. Return again to the initial mantra, "I love myself because I am a son/daughter of God."

Realize you are lovable and have worth because God created you, and hence, this is the core essence of who and what you really are. It is really only society's programming that teaches us there is something that we have to do to be lovable and have worth. We are all diamonds with mud on us, and with the mud being negative-ego programming, it is our job to cleanse it away and replace it with the oversoul's more christed way of thinking.

Then let the words go and simply follow the breath. Give yourself a great big hug; wait until you are ready to get up and then do so.

This is also a wonderful way to drift off to sleep at night because it leaves the subconscious mind imprinted with self-love.

This meditation, although quite simple, is a very powerful tool in re-programming the subconscious mind and the inner child that thinks itself unworthy of self-love. This meditation puts your conscious mind and higher self in charge, rather than allowing others, your lower self or the subconscious mind to control you. You are in essence telling your inner child and subconscious mind that which is truth. You might have been living through the faulty belief that denies you the love you seek, but know that that is merely the voice of the negative ego. The voice of the higher self and monad is the voice of truth and that aspect of self does love you because you are. Therefore, there is no deception going on in this meditation, but the affirmation of the higher self to the subconscious mind that it loves itself and therefore *you*, because you are part and parcel of its divine being. Or, put another way, you are loved because you are a son/daughter of God.

The key understanding here is that there are really only two voices or two philosophies of life in every person that are diametrically opposed. There is the philosophy and attitude system of the oversoul, monad and God and that of the lower self and/or negative ego. One is truth and one is illusion. The law of the mind, however, is that your thoughts create your reality. If you let the negative ego and lower self be your teacher and guide as opposed to the higher self and God, you will live in a self-created hell of your own thought creation. The subconscious mind, having no reasoning and being basically just a computer, will repeat back anything you allow to be programmed into it. This is why it is essential to be vigilant over your own thought process and what you allow to be programmed into you by other people. The good news is it takes only twenty-one days to cement a new habit into the subconscious mind. In essence it is just a process of denial and affirmation. Deny the negative thought forms and affirmations of the negative ego from entering your mind and replace them with the thought form, affirmations and visualizations of the truth that the oversoul, monad and mighty I Am Presence would have you see.

No Comparing or Competing

Our world still operates on the basis of comparison and competition, and this means that we need to rally all the forces within us to go against the common tide. We are each unique individuals with particular strengths and particular areas that need strengthening, but we are here to work on ourselves and not to compare ourselves with others. Unfortunately, most of us have received messages to the contrary, and from early childhood on have found ourselves in a state of comparison and competition. It is okay to compare with oneself, but it is the negative ego that makes up comparisons with others.

Fortunately, the world is slowly but surely moving away from this type of thinking, with more progressive schools and more people becoming aware of the higher self and the greater purposes of life. If we can find those special schools for our children and find a community of spiritually and psychologically aware people with whom we can interact, the easier the process of our own transformation will become. The truth is, however, that we all must begin with where we find ourselves, both in our own inner as well as outer worlds. The work of transformation, initiation and ascension begins with each of us individually as we do our part to the best of our ability. As we begin to change within, we will find that the outer support we are seeking will either find us or call to us to come join them. The work of the moment needs to be done in the moment, and therefore let us begin here and now to stop all comparisons and competitions with one another. The following are some tools and ideas for how this can be achieved.

Chart of Comparisons

Begin by making a simple chart listing all those areas where you find that you judge and compare yourself to others most harshly. Some examples are:

- Feeling fatter than him/her,
- Feeling intellectually inferior to him/her,
- Not attractive enough to be loved by them,
- Not having the career that he/she does,
- Ashamed of health lessons because others don't have them.

Using this as a basic model, list any that for you are areas where you deem yourself unworthy of your God-given heritage and right to self-love by virtue of faulty comparative thinking.

Then each day, on a rating scale of one to ten, with ten being the most self-love you have achieved in these areas, fill in the appropriate number that you feel indicates the letting go of comparing so you can love yourself. Not all the issues that you write down will come up during a given day, so you might want to put in the date of your entry. As you continue working, this simple chart will highlight the areas where self-love is being withheld due to faulty comparative thinking. The more awareness you have about this issue, the higher the numbers will grow. It is an interesting phenomenon that simply by drawing your attention to these areas and actually seeing in black and white the points where you are weakest and where you're willing to rate yourself on a daily basis, you will gain enormous strength and make a great deal of progress. All this will be achieved by faithfully working this chart. This technique is also called keeping a spiritual log and accounting of your character development.

Chart of Competitions

In a similar fashion, many of us become victims of the competition factor. It would likewise be worth your while to make a chart based on your competitions with others. The following is an example of how to create a chart or log of this nature.

There are (any number you choose) areas in which I find myself in competition with others. These are the ones that need the most attention:

- Jane Doe is much better at finances than I am.
- I'll never be as pretty/good looking as so and so.
- I don't keep my home as spotless as so and so.
- My car looks like it belongs in the dump heap, and I find myself competing to have a nicer car than my friends (or other cars on the road).
- My workout at the gym is lame and I'll never compete with the rest of the group.
- I'm so ungraceful doing yoga posture; how can I compete with them?
- I'm losing my hair, getting older, not as well-dressed as so and so.

You can see what I'm getting at here. Then follow the same rating system you did in the previous chart and see how much more confident you grow in these areas as well. Just by bringing this to your awareness, your belief systems will change. When you see the amount of low self-esteem you are perpetuating by unconsciously living these destructive patterns on a daily basis, you will have the conscious mind's and higher self's attention. Then these patterns will automatically begin to shift from the unconscious mind playing them out to the conscious mind and higher self healing them.

Once you are working at the conscious and subconscious reprogramming of your faulty belief system in comparisons and competitions, you will be on the way to traversing interconnected roadblocks to unconditional self-love, peace and personal empowerment. So much of our development into integrated, healthy, psychologically free and spiritually uplifted individuals lies in the awareness of what the subconscious mind and inner child are holding as a belief system. Once this is done, we have the opportunity to work with our conscious minds, higher selves, monads and masters to gain mastery in these areas. Again, it's a process of denying the faulty thought form and replacing it with the opposite affirmation that your higher self would have you program your subconscious mind with.

Asking the Masters to Aid in the Self-Love Process

The final technique I share with you for developing self-love uses the masters themselves to help fill you with their blessed divine energy. Personally, I find that working with both God and the masters, as well as with the conscious mind and higher self, is the best all-around program for healing any pattern of faulty thinking or negativity.

Technique for Healing Faulty Thinking

1. *Assume a relaxed position, either lying down or seated (be sure the spine is straight and the legs are uncrossed except when sitting in a yoga posture).*
2. *Take a few deep, long but comfortable breaths, allowing the body to relax to greater degrees with each breath.*
3. *Then allow the body to simply relax into its position, as you follow the natural flow of breath.*
4. *Think either upon God as pure love or upon one of the masters with whom you feel a particular connection in the energies of unconditional love. Some masters I find particularly helpful are Jesus/Sananda, Sai Baba, Lord Maitreya/Christ/Krishna, beloved Mother Mary, Quan Yin, master Kuthumi and Djwhal Khul. Of course, these examples are not meant to limit you in any way because the possibilities are endless. They are just a few of those particular masters whom I find myself personally connected with when working with the specific energy of love.*
5. *Once you have found the master upon whom you wish to meditate, call to him/her either silently or aloud, asking him to fill you with the divine energy of unconditional love.*
6. *Focus on his presence as if being held within the cave of the heart,*

there to expand like a blossoming flower.

7. *Allow yourself to focus jointly upon the third eye, while quietly calling the master's energy into the heart area. This will link both heart and mind/visualization in a joint process of invocation.*

8. *Relax deeper and simply seek to feel his divine presence.*

9. *Imagine that you are breathing in and out of the heart area as though your nose was located at the heart center, and then just relax into the inbreath, the outbreath and that place in between.*

10. *Focus solely on feeling the energies of unconditional love flooding your entire being.*

11. *While doing this, allow yourself to merge with the feeling of love, until you, the master and/or God are one, blended in the energies of unconditional love.*

12. *Stay in that place as long as is comfortable, allowing it to permeate every cell of your being. Let it flow from the tip of your toes to the top of your head. Let it flow also from your higher self and conscious awareness to your subconscious mind. Let it bathe the inner child in the aura of divine love and protection.*

13. *When you feel ready to come out of this meditation, thank both God and the masters for their help. Then begin once more to simply follow the natural flow of the breath.*

14. *When you feel ready, either slowly arise from this state of relaxation or meditation to continue with your day, or allow yourself to drift off to sleep, knowing that you have been blessed with love divine from God, the master(s) and your own higher self.*

If you do go about your day following such a meditation, remember to hold that energy within you as a precious gift that has been given. Remember also that it is a gift upon which both you and the masters can continue to build and enhance, so that ultimately you yourself are a perfect manifestation of the divine love of God on Earth.

Owning Your Own Personal Power

One of the most important tools and keys to the psychology of ascension is owning your own personal power. In fact, the ability to unconditionally love both self and others forms a type of spiritual marriage with the ability to own your own personal power. These qualities form two halves of one whole and are of vital import when taking various initiations and completing your ascension process. Both these aspects of self must be under the control of the conscious mind. Like the aspect of love, the owning of one's personal power is a process that you may as well begin starting to work on now, since it is an attitude that must be held in ever-greater degrees as you proceed with future initiations. As the adage goes, "There's no time like the present," so let us begin exploring this area.

As I discussed earlier, from the time we enter this world we are being affected by the belief systems of others. This process begins with the attitude of doctors, nurses or midwives who help us and our mothers with the birthing process, and continues with the programming of our parents' belief systems. In most cases, they who raised us continued in the tradition of the negative-ego faulty belief system with which they were raised, imparting these impressions during the earliest and most vulnerable times of our lives.

This conditioning was carried on in the schools we attended, within our group of friends and more likely than not, into our jobs or career choices. Adding to this programming, we are continuously bombarded with impressions from newspapers, magazines, television and films, influencing us in a less-than-spiritual mode of thinking (and that's putting it mildly).

Therefore it becomes imperative that once we become conscious of treading the path of initiation and ascension we learn how to claim the personal power of our own free will and retrain ourselves to think with the spiritual, or christed, mind. The difference between the two modes of thinking is like the difference between night and day. I guarantee you, however, that once the higher self is guiding us, we will finally know ourselves to be the glorious beings that we are, and we can remain calm and unruffled in all circumstances that come our way. This is because from the higher lens, life's challenges will be viewed as lessons to be learned and mastered, rather than as bad luck or "bummers." The peace of mind everyone on Earth is seeking lies in maintaining the proper perspective and interpretation in all situations. It is a matter of asking yourself, Is the glass of water half empty or half full? We don't see only with our physical eyes but also with our minds.

We are attempting to reprogram the subconscious mind so that we are the masters of it, rather than the other way around. This will have the double effect of being in the driver's seat in terms of thought patterns that arise both from within our subconscious minds and from well-meaning (or not-so-well-meaning) friends and/or society in general.

To begin with, you must first recognize and affirm that your personal power lies within you. It is, in truth, part of your divine makeup and heritage. What you need to do, right from the moment when you first realize that fact (which I trust is now), is claim it! Claim that power upon awakening every morning. Take a moment at noon and afternoon to claim it again, and then certainly claim it for your own before bed each night. Whenever a particularly challenging situation arises—at the workplace, within your family structure or anywhere—reclaim that you are the master of your domain and have total access to your personal power. It is one hundred percent up to you what you choose to let into your conscious mind. Simply refuse to take in anything that is less than divine. In this manner your progress will ultimately be speeded up a thousandfold, and the very pattern of your thinking will be changed forever.

Diffusing Others' Negativity

That we each have the power to render other people's negativity powerless over us might seem impossible but this power lies within all of us. The way other people's negative belief systems affect us seems quite overpowering at times, and I can understand doubts you might have. With proper understanding, guidance and the claiming of our own personal power, however, this mastery can ultimately be achieved.

First, be aware of how susceptible we are in general to the slightest suggestion of negativity from other people. Take, for example, the person who walks into the workplace feeling quite healthy, only to be met by a fellow employee who tells him/her that she doesn't look well and asks if anything is the matter. The reply is a hesitant "no," immediately followed by a trip to the bathroom mirror and an in-depth investigation of skin tone, throat, tongue and forehead temperature. If this examination convinces her that she's healthy, then she proceeds with the day. However, there will most likely be a periodic testing of muscles for aches and pains and a general observation of skin tone throughout the remainder of the day. If another person comes up with this same observation, you can bet that our hapless worker will think she *must* be ill, and by the third time (perhaps based on a less-than-flattering shirt color chosen that day), might actually start running a raging fever. Now, I say this with a twist of levity, but the sad fact is that these situations often arise, and many a healthy person winds up in a sickbed due to a poor clothing choice. And this because she allowed herself to be victimized and hypnotized by another person's negative suggestion. You don't have to go to a licensed hypnotist to get hypnotized, for until lessons are mastered it happens moment by moment in our daily lives. The subconscious mind, having no reasoning, is easily programmed by whatever suggestion or thought you, the conscious mind, allow into it from within or from others.

If we are, as a species, so very vulnerable, what then to do with the vast amounts of negativity encountered (both on the home front and out in the world) during the course of any given day? The answer is to claim our own personal power, rather than be re-actors to the negativity, suggestions and stresses around us. The ideal is to respond rather than react. To respond is to come from the conscious mind. To react is to come from the subconscious mind and often the negative ego.

Maintaining a steady claim on one's personal power requires much vigilance, and I am not suggesting that it is by any means easy. But I am suggesting that it is possible and doable and that there are those of us who have done this to varying degrees. There are many of us who have been working long and hard at claiming our own personal power and in blending our will with the will of God and the masters. It becomes easier as time goes on because you have trained yourself to come from this new center.

Some of us will find this more of a challenge than others, since we each have our own particular weaknesses and strengths. Also, some of us find ourselves in more challenging environments—a bad marriage, a terminally ill relative, acute financial lessons or extremely stressful job situations. The first thing I would ask you to do if you find yourself in this category is to look at your situation as holding a wonderful opportunity to practice throwing off the negativity of others and holding the light and positivity in that situation. By doing this, you are reframing your situation. Instead of looking at it in the light of "poor little me," you are looking at it through the lens of opportunity. This readjustment of thinking, in psychological terms, is called reframing. You are also looking at the situation as a spiritual test of your mastery and your Christ/spiritual consciousness.

The actual practice of using one's personal will power to keep other people's negativity at bay is the same for all of us. It involves affirming our own power and the healthy denial of anyone else's power over us. One of my personal phrases when practicing this is "other people's negativity rolls off me like water off a duck's back." That keeps it simple, but gets right to the point.

Another favorite practice is to see myself surrounded by a semipermeable bubble of golden white light. I affirm that only that which is good and of God is allowed through this bubble. All that is not of the highest is kept out of this bubble of light. I find this particularly helpful when negative words and/or energies are flying about. For those in the bigger cities, this might occur in a traffic jam, riding the subways or just walking the streets. As a rule, I always try to surround myself with kindred spirits who are themselves working on bringing forth the highest within them. But even in these situations there is the potential for someone's negative ego to come bursting through his/her usually calm demeanor. In such an instance, I quickly put up my golden white bubble of protection, affirm my own personal power and remind myself that other people's negative emotions roll off me like water off a duck's back. This technique can help a person on the path of ascension through many a holiday gathering with family and friends.

I suggest that you never leave home without first clothing or surrounding yourself with this bubble of protection. Likewise, do at least one affirmation that claims your own power of will. Lastly, find a little phrase to your own liking, such as my duck phrase, that you can say to yourself when surrounded by a field of negative thoughts, emotions or energy. Some alternate suggestions are: "I remain an undisturbed pool of pure, still water, unmoved by the storms about me;" "I am calm and smooth as pure, uncut marble;" or "I am a firm, immovable mountain." Find whatever does the trick for you. Remember that practice makes perfect, and that once you have invoked your will there is nothing to stop you from claiming your personal power and maintaining it at all times. Always remember, it is your thoughts that cause your reality. After you put on your mental clothing each morning, also call to God and the masters for their protection, as well. The key understanding here is that it is your job to establish your psychological immune system, and God and the masters will then supply added support. This is a two-pronged approach; asking only the masters or God to do it will not work. Each mind—subconscious, conscious and superconscious—has its part to play. As the saying goes, "God helps those who help themselves."

Conscious Control over the Subconscious Mind

In reprogramming and assuming mastery, the things we need to be the most watchful of are not what comes from other people, places or things, but rather what comes from our own subconscious mind. It is ultimately the subconscious mind and inner child from which the automatic reactions come. And if we truly want to act rather than react from negative beliefs, we must take full charge, using the power of personal will, conscious mind, God and the masters to change these faulty patterns that haunt most of our subconscious minds.

The good news is that we *can* do this. In actuality, the subconscious mind is like a computer, storing what is put into it and printing it out on the screens of our lives, usually to our detriment. This same computer, with the right programming, can and will play back the most positive images and messages if that is what we put into it. The subconscious mind is just as happy to form a positive habit as it is a negative one. It is the job of the conscious mind to be the computer programmer. Just as when dealing with external negative influences, we have the same ability to change the programming and totally restructure both what is already within the subconscious mind and certainly what we put into it from this moment forward.

You must acknowledge that you and your conscious mind are masters of this inner realm. You can then begin to restructure that subconscious mind so that it reflects the highest of which you are capable at any given time. The higher self and the masters are awaiting your call to bring forth the greatest good, and their help can be invaluable as a support to your conscious work.

One of the most powerful tools for reprogramming the subconscious mind is the use of positive affirmations. These can be self-created or selected from a wide range of tapes available in your local metaphysical bookstore. Said aloud each day, affirmations inform the computer system within that you are whole, powerful, strong, an invincible son/daughter of God, unaffected by old faulty belief systems and so forth. Like a hungry computer, the subconscious mind will feed upon these new messages, and over a given period of time, these new positive messages will replace the old negative ones. (Again, it takes twenty-one days to cement a new habit into the subconscious mind.)

If you do buy audio tapes (and there are some wonderful ones on the market), you can play them in a restful state and the effect will be quite monumental. The period when you are drifting off to sleep is one of the most significant doorways into the subconscious, and it is suggested that you begin to play these tapes when you are tired and ready for sleep. If you have a tape recorder with auto-reverse, these affirmations will float you off to sleep in a state of positivity and will then be fed into your subconscious mind throughout the night. This is a wonderful way to overhaul your personal computer. I am not saying to do this every single night, but in the beginning while you are working at changing the basic habit and patterns of your subconscious thinking, it is advisable to do this for a twenty-one day period. And all you have to do is simply turn the tape on and fall asleep.

You can create a tape or a tape series yourself. Because the tape is in your own voice, it will be the conscious part of you talking to the subconscious part of you, which creates an added impact. You would then have the ability to tailor these tapes to focus specifically on areas on which you want to work. This is not necessary, however. It is merely offered as an alternative suggestion to those who have both the time and inclination to create such tapes.

In *Soul Psychology* I offer a variety of techniques for working with the subconscious mind. You might want to add some of those tools to the list given here. There are also many affirmations for working on personal power, self-love, protection and healing in general.

Here is a sample meditation you can do to reprogram the subconscious with the help of God and the masters.

Meditation for Reprogramming the Subconscious

1. *Assume a position of relaxation, either lying down or seated (remember to keep the spine erect and the legs uncrossed, unless in the traditional yoga posture).*
2. *Take a few deep, long breaths, allowing the body to relax ever more with each breath.*

3. *Allow the body to relax into its position, following the natural flow of the breath.*

4. *Think upon God or one of the masters with whom you feel a particular connection in the area of will and/or strength. (A wonderful master to call in this regard is El Morya, as he is chohan of the first ray, the ray of will. Other masters with whom you might want to work are Archangel Michael, Saint Germain, Sai Baba and Jesus/Sananda.*

5. *Call to the master silently or aloud, asking him/her to fill you with the divine energy of will. Tell him that you want this energy to fill your entire being, as well as to reprogram your subconscious mind with the belief system of personal power, strength and will.*

6. *Focus on the master's presence at the point midway between the eyebrow (third-eye area) and the top of the head.*

7. *Allow yourself to use the joined energies of the third eye and the top of the head to feel the pulsating power of will.*

8. *Relax deeper while you feel the power of the master's divine will flood your conscious and subconscious mind, adding this will to your own and gifting you with the power over your subconscious mind that you seek.*

9. *Imagine that you are breathing in and out of the third-eye area as if it has a nose, and then just relax into the inbreath, the outbreath and that place in between.*

10. *Let this particular time be focused solely on feeling the energies of will, strength, power and purpose as they flood your entire being.*

11. *While doing this, allow yourself to merge with the feeling of will, until you, the master, and/or God are one, being blended in the energies of pure will itself.*

12. *Stay in that place as long as is comfortable, allowing it to permeate every cell of your being. Let it flow from the tip of your toes to the top of your head. Let it also flow from your higher self and conscious awareness into your subconscious mind. Let it bathe the subconscious mind and inner child with the knowingness that you are all powerful and a being blessed with divine will power.*

13. *When you are ready to come out of this meditation, thank both God and the master(s) for their help. Then begin once more to simply follow the natural flow of the breath.*

14. *When you feel ready, either slowly arise from this state of relaxation and meditation to continue with your day, or allow yourself to drift off to sleep, knowing that you have been immersed in and reprogrammed with the will of God.*

If you do go about the day after such a meditation, remember to hold that energy and attitude within you, so that both you and the master(s) can keep building, enhancing and furthering that aspect of will and reprogramming of your subconscious mind to know you are a perfect manifestation of the will of God on Earth.

One reminder: First, claim your personal power consciously on the psychological level. Then do the above meditation, which will support the claim of your one hundred percent power that you have created for yourself. Finally, your personal power, although claimed one hundred percent, can be used only for unconditional love and not for control or negative manipulation of others.

The Marriage of Love and Will

It must be understood that love and will must be integrated in a type of divine alchemical marriage within the initiate. Just as love and light are generally seen as two halves of one whole, so must love and will within the divine triad of light, love and will be seen as a coupling unto themselves.

The will of humanity is vital to both initiation and ascension, as well as in one's own personal psychology, which truly cannot rightly be seen as separate from the path of initiation. Therefore, the cultivation of willpower or one's own personal power extends from the subconscious depths of mind all the way through and ultimately beyond the seven levels of initiation—ascension itself. In the alchemy of the marriage divine, however, will without love is like the groom without the bride. Will, in fact, is generally thought of as a masculine principle; whereas love is generally thought of as a feminine principle. Light/wisdom falls somewhat androgynously between the two.

Let us look at the importance of will and love functioning together as a unit. The will aspect gives love the strength from which to operate. The love aspect gives to will the heart needed in the application of will. Will without heart can easily manifest as cold and uncaring power. Love without will and strength can float about limply and hazily, without force or direction. But when the two are properly integrated and functioning as one, it makes for the perfect expression of God on Earth.

When dealing specifically with the psychology of ascension and the healthy reprogramming of an initiate's, or any person's, subconscious mind and emotions, the balance between the two are of utmost importance. What we are seeking to achieve is an integrated, whole, healthy and fully rounded individual; one who is able to function equally out of heart and head. The perfect balance, therefore, becomes mandatory. And into this balance we must likewise add the light/wisdom aspect of God and human.

The Divine Triad of Light, Love and Power (Will)

Before concluding this chapter on the psychology of ascension, we must address the function of light. It is interesting that when discussing the ascension process, most lightworkers (as initiates are now commonly called) focus first and primarily upon the aspect of light. There is great, and appropriate interest in raising the light quotient (amount of light) that one carries within the four-body system. However, I choose to include it last in this chapter, because as one evolves in the realms of love, will and wisdom, the light is automatically brought through.

I am by no means saying that specific meditations and activations on raising the light within oneself should be de-emphasized. I am saying only that all these aspects need to form an integrated whole within the life of all who embrace the path of ascension.

In another sense, all that has been offered in this book falls under the category of light. Another name for light is wisdom, and through the information in this book I have sought to impart wisdom and therefore light unto you. For without the light of wisdom, there would be no understanding of either love or will. Therefore, please bear in mind that light has flooded and lighted every word upon these pages.

All planes of being are composed of light, from the densest of material worlds through the logoic, or seventh, plane where we attain our full ascension and beyond into the 352 levels of the godhead. The denser the matter, the slower the light particles vibrate. The more refined the matter of a realm or body, the faster and brighter the light particles vibrate. The fact remains, however, that all is light.

It is by the direct knowing of this that certain masters (if it is or has been their specific mission) are able to effectuate so-called miracles. What they are doing in essence, is completely identifying with the light that they are, so that from this place of oneness with the light, they can manipulate the particles of light, which we on Earth perceive to be dense matter. Examples of this include the miracles of Jesus Christ, where water was turned to wine, a few loaves of bread and a handful of fish were multiplied to feed thousands, the turbulent seas were calmed at his command and the multitude of healings that he performed (light, love and will were all involved in these processes).

Another example of this type of light manipulation is occurring on a daily basis through the power and love of Sai Baba, an avatar in India. This being is healing the sick, raising the dead and manifesting blessed objects out of the ethers for his devotees, including holy ash known as *virbhuti*, which he creates with a wave of his hand. He lives in a small village called Putaparti, where throngs of people go to see him. He visits those he chooses all around the globe by virtue of his ability to manifest his body of light anywhere, at anytime. There are Sai Baba centers around the globe filled with devotees who have direct experience of his miracles. He says that he performs these miracles for the sole purpose of demonstrating God on Earth, and I myself have been personally touched by his grace and benediction. I cannot recommend strongly enough researching and seeking out this divine avatar (one who is born God realized). *The Complete Ascension Manual* has a chapter dedicated to him, and there are books by Howard Murphet recounting his, as well as others personal experiences with Sai Baba. I have, myself, dedicated a book to this remarkable man of miracles. In *Golden Keys to Ascension and Healing*, I tell of his bountiful grace, wisdom and love I have experienced. In truth, all that needs to be said about the holy triad of light, love and power (will) can be summed up in the name and life of Sai Baba.

Conclusion

I hope that this chapter will impart to the new seeker, as well as to those who are quite advanced initiates, the importance of full integration on all levels. For the beginning initiate, the sooner you begin to work on the healing, purifying and cleansing of the lower four bodies, the faster you will evolve through your initiatory process. To the advanced initiate, even if you have indeed reached the seventh level of initiation, the clearer you are psychologically, the clearer a channel you will be for the full manifestation of the light, love and power that you are.

Ultimately, each of us at every single level and at every step of the way must keep purifying and holding ourselves in a state of balance. Some who are more advanced might have a bit of catch-up work to do, but that's all right too, for we have achieved anchoring the light on the Earth that was our destiny, and we continue in that vein. Likewise we have achieved our ascension in anchoring this divine light. The fact remains that we now have a bit of cleanup or balancing work to do in our psychological selves in order to manifest more fully that light and find the appropriate blend of the light, love and power, which we indeed embody and which in fact has allowed us to achieve our ascension into light. The key point I'm making is that you can pass or achieve high levels of initiation while still having enormous amounts of psychological unclarity. Just because you are, for example, a seventh-degree initiate, does not mean that you are fully manifesting God in your mental, emotional, etheric or physical bodies.

This is an extremely important point for advanced lightworkers to understand. The high level of initiation has more to do with the amount of light quotient you are holding, rather than psychospiritual and character development. All lightworkers who have not mastered the psychological level of the path of ascension will remain stuck in their evolutionary-initiation process until this level is mastered to a satisfactory degree in the eyes of the masters. A full-fledged ascended master demonstrates godliness not just in the light or initiation he/she holds, but also in his mastery and proper integration of mind, emotion, physical body, relationship interactions, environment, psychology, wisdom, service work, love quotient, transcendence of negative ego, demonstration of Christ consciousness and spiritual leadership. When all these aspects of self are properly integrated, synthesized and mastered to a high degree, then and only then can one truly be seen and recognized as a full-fledged ascended master. And this applies to every initiate on Earth and on the inner plane, regardless of his/her level of initiation. It is not perfection that is required, but rather a high degree or percentage of mastery in these areas.

The process of initiation and ascension is an eternal process, for God is limitless and none of us can possibly limit that which is limitless by nature. Therefore, let us proceed to do the work at hand and continue fine-tuning this glorious process in order to serve the One of which we are all one. And let us cultivate patience in our work, for eternity has all the time in the world.

5

The Question of Karma
The Law of Cause and Effect

I begin this chapter with a quote from the Kybalion: "Every cause has its effect; every effect has its cause; everything happens according to law; chance is but a name for law not recognized; there are many planes of causation, but nothing escapes the law." I find this particular quotation to express the teachings of beloved master Jesus: "As ye sow, so shall ye reap," albeit with a bit more of an esoteric/scientific perspective. Both these teachings express what in Eastern tradition is simply called karma.

The most basic explanation for karma is, as stated so eloquently above, cause and effect. We are not victims of a random universe, but are cocreators with God, given the reign of free choice. Along with this power of free choice comes the law of consequence. Every action we take, every thought we think, every deed we do hold within them the seeds for manifestation that will outpicture within our lives.

Karma as Motive

We are, at every moment of our existence, creating the next moment by how we are conducting ourselves in the present. This conduct applies to motive and intent to an even greater degree than it does to the form of any given expression. I do not mean that we are not accountable for our deeds, but that we are judged to a greater degree by the laws of life based on the motivation of our actions than by any specific action itself.

Take, for example, the person who is a great benefactor to the poor who does this to gain public recognition, fame, respect and power, rather than out of any real concern for the people being helped. Of course, this person would accumulate some measure of good karma for the deeds rendered, but because the motive is selfish, the amount of good that he/she would build up in his life would be limited. Compare that person with a struggling person who really feels for those less fortunate than herself and in turn donates, recycles and tithes the little she has. The motive of that person would be pure and truly altruistic and the good karma thus accumulated would be great indeed.

Therefore, karma is a very subtle issue and not one that can be easily seen through the outer eye. Doing good for its own sake is of far greater value than doing good to simply look good in the eyes of one's peers or society in general. Examine the motives of all that you do, for ultimately it is by motive and intent that we create the reality within which we live.

Karma as Lessons

Karma, then, is the result of a cause set in motion by an individual, a group of individuals, a specific culture or, indeed, by the planet as a whole. Often the term "karma" is used to mean only the negative outpicturing of events, but this is not true. Karma is simply the appropriate effect of any given cause, both positive and/or negative, and it is the ultimate teacher of lessons. That which we call bad or negative karma is actually a movement set in motion by the law of life to propel us into the appropriate experience where the next lesson we need to learn awaits us. If not to our liking, we will generally call this bad karma; but if we explore this a little further, we can see that that is not the case at all.

Suppose we have been judgmental of those who seem subject to a fragile nature, considering them weak for getting sick all the time. Perhaps we do this because we were born with a sturdy constitution, strongly built, or perhaps have worked though a large measure of physical-plane weakness during a previous incarnation. On the other hand, we have sensitivities that await our future development, certain sensitivities that will be vital to our spiritual growth and render *us* a bit more delicate in the eyes of the world. If we continually judge our brothers and sisters for having to deal with certain physical or health lessons, rest assured that we ourselves will be subjected to a similar situation whether or not this was what destiny had in mind for us.

We will be made to face that which we judged, lashed out against, condemned, abused, misused, took advantage of and so forth, in order to experience what it is like so we may become truly compassionate beings. It is hoped that we will learn from our God-given qualities of reason, compassion, light, love and wisdom. If we do not, then karma will certainly put us right in the middle of a situation where we cannot help but learn the required lesson. And if we do not learn that lesson at once, karma will keep placing us into ever-deeper levels of that particular lesson until we finally do get it. It must be understood that even bad karma is a gift, not a punishment. It is teaching us an important lesson we need to learn. The ideal, however, is to learn by grace or the easy way, instead of the school of hard knocks that forces us to learn a spiritual lesson we have been resisting.

Positive Karma

Karma can be quite positive, carrying us with joy into realms of the most wondrous experience. If we take a moment to consider the axioms "every cause has its effect" and "as ye sow, so shall ye reap," we can see that this river of karma flows both ways. It is as much the outpicturing of the good we have done in our lives as it is the negative paths we have taken. It serves as much as a reinforcer of the positive as it does an instructor through the harsher experiences of our lives. This is often overlooked.

Let us look at how some positive karma finds its way into manifestation in our lives. To begin with, if we truly follow the example in the phrase, "as ye sow, so shall ye reap," we can easily see that what we are doing throughout our lives is planting the seeds of future manifestation. First, we plant these karmic seeds within our own auric fields, where they find residence in what is occultly called the permanent atoms. I shall explain more about this, but suffice it to say that we magnetize ourselves by what we have put out into the world and shall attract back to us that which we have given forth.

Each of us, therefore, carries the magnetism, or radiance, of all the good actions and pure motivations of everything that we have put forth in all our previous lives. Thus, all acts of kindness, generosity, love, charity, forgiveness and so forth will blossom forth in subsequent lives. Those whose vision extends only to the one life they are living and who imagine their existence will go no further often see life as dealing them, or others, a raw deal. My beloved readers, this is not so. If one has given of himself/herself with purity of motive and heart or has sacrificed his personal life for the greater ideal, such as in the case of a dedicated soul who dies without friends, finances or recognition, please know that neither he nor you simply fade into the abyss, unrewarded or truly unrecognized.

In such cases, there is a particular lesson that the soul had to learn by experiencing such a lifetime, but all the good done is recorded within the permanent atoms, or aura, and will attract in succeeding lifetimes the fruits of his/her good works. Thus you might see, by your limited vision, a person who is born with a "silver spoon in his mouth" and believe his good fortune is an injustice to you if you are working through a life of particular struggle and hardship. This person, however, has earned the situation into which he/she was born by virtue of his good karma. For nothing in life, when viewed through the greater lens of God, is either haphazard or unfair. Now, the person born with good karma has free choice in how he uses his good fortune. He can use his wealth in service and for the spiritual and physical upliftment of humanity or he can use it selfishly. It is always hoped that we all learn from grace and that the rich increase their wealth in spiritual service, but this is not always the case. They will, however, still have the opportunity to reap the good that they have sown in a previous incarnation before being called to task if the choices they make in their present incarnation are selfish and hurtful.

Karma is a constantly flowing stream, carrying upon its current both the negative and positive outpicturing of situations and events that are seen through a glass darkly, when viewed only from a third-dimensional perspective. Trust me when I tell you that they who seem lucky in love, blessed with good health, born with extreme physical beauty and born into loving and supportive families have within the scope of their many incarnations earned that destiny. They are only chosen who themselves first choose. Yet, dear readers, there remains one vital key that is missing from this equation. We must realize that, from our three-dimensional vantage point, we cannot truly tell the easier road from the more difficult.

Judge Not, Lest You Judge in Error

It is natural to look upon one who from an earthly perspective seemingly has everything and think of him/her as lucky. It is natural to wish we were in that person's place. But let me tell you, both from the spiritual vantage point and from the perspective of one who has lived for some time in Los Angeles (the city of the rich and famous), that to covet our neighbor's life, were we to get it, would turn out to be the biggest mistake of our lives! Never forget the biblical adage, "What profit a man if he gain the whole world and lose his own soul?" Many who are not rich in their finances are indeed rich in the accumulated good karma of their soul body, which is destined to lead to material prosperity as well.

Karma is one of the most intricate facets of God. What seems to be positive can be is the most difficult of pathways. What, from the outside, appears to contain all the goodies that life can offer, is very often the lesson of just how hollow and empty a life without God first truly is. I am not saying that this is the case for everyone with the goodies, for indeed there are some incredibly beautiful souls who have dedicated their outer success to uplifting humanity and furthering the development of the kingdoms of God upon this Earth. What I am trying to convey is just how tricky a rascal karma can be. The best approach to this most mysterious of God's aspects is to live in a state of the highest attunement possible, and come what may, stay ever steady upon your spiritual path.

I once heard a story, the source of which I cannot now recall, but the teaching of it is quite applicable. It is actually a parable on karma, and it goes something like the this:

A couple was feeling lonely and prayed to God for a son. The couple was granted a son and began a great celebration.

"You are so fortunate to have born a child this late in life," said a neighbor.

"In the father's stead, a wise man answered with the simple reply, "Maybe."

Time passed, and the child grew into a young man and wanted a horse. Having little money, the parents prayed hard and sincerely for a horse for their son. God granted this request. The father rejoiced, saying how fortunate they were and how kind God had again been to him.

And the wise man responded as he did before, with the simple injunction, "Maybe."

A few weeks later the son was out riding and had a terrible accident, being thrown from the horse and breaking several ribs and both legs. The father responded by admonishing God for suddenly being so cruel and unjust.

The wise man, who was never very far from the family, simply responded as always, with a half-smile from the corner of his mouth, "Maybe."

The son lay injured, fighting for his life, when a war broke out. All the other young men in the village went off to fight this war and, with the odds against them, were all killed in battle. Meanwhile, the son made miraculous strides in his recovery. The father now said how kind God was in injuring his son so that ultimately his life was spared.

And the wise man simply smiled his half-smile and replied, "Maybe."

There is no end to this parable. It simply shows the currents of karma and our ultimate inability to discern what is good karma and what is so-called bad karma. For this reason, I urge you to look at karma as lessons and just keep on keeping on. Until you have the ability to stay in constant contact with your higher self or monad and refrain from limited perceptions of things, my advice to you all is to go through your karmic lessons as graciously as possible. And with the half-smile of the wise one, judge it not, but simply reply, "Maybe," to those who would judge it either good or bad and leave the rest to God.

An Esoteric Look at Karma

It is an esoteric fact that everything we say, think, do, feel and experience is recorded. This has been sensed and spoken of by almost all religions. This truth, however, has been held up as a threat to the participants of these various paths, rather than revealed as a tool of growth and understanding. Therefore, as we move deeper into the study of this wisdom, I ask you to remove the lens of judgment and replace it with the lenses of compassion for self and humanity. As I said, karma, most simply put, is the law of cause and effect and the tool by which needed lessons are learned. Viewed from the higher self/monad, it carries with it no judgment, but is seen as law in action, propelling us forward to deeper wisdom and God-attuned action.

It is with this lens that I seek to reveal some of the more esoteric workings of this law. The appropriate response to all karma, be it good, bad or maybe, is "Not my will but thine; thank you for the lesson." This attitude allows one to work with the universe and learn from it. Fighting the universe creates perpetual anger and being upset. A helpful way to look at this is to see everything that happens as a spiritual test that teaches you self-mastery and the ability to retain the Christ consciousness in all situations. One other extremely helpful attitude is having preferences in life, not attachments. A preference is an attitude of wanting something, but still being happy if you don't get it. An attachment attitude, however, leaves you disappointed, bummed out and angry when your desires are not met. This additional teaching will help you learn to see life through your christ eyes rather than the negative ego's eyes.

The Permanent Atoms

There are, within each of the four lower bodies, that which is known as the *permanent atoms*. These minute recording structures bear the imprint of our lives throughout all our incarnations. Upon our transition to the inner worlds, these atoms are held in a sort of stasis and are called forth in the building process of our four lower bodies when we next incarnate. They are therefore not a means by which a cruel and callous God judges us. Rather, they are a means by which we are each afforded the God-given right, and even power, to access our own growth patterns, as well as alter them. In this way we may produce both cause and effect ever more representative of the sons and daughters of God, which we all are.

When someone crosses over to the inner planes, he/she finds himself on a world most attuned and harmonious to the basic core structure of the lives he has outpictured upon the Earth. This is due, in great part, to the effect of the permanent atoms. Since these atoms are not destroyed, but are the foundation upon which we build our future incarnations, it makes sense that both the permanent atoms of the astral and mental vehicles will likewise carry us into the appropriate astral and mental realms of divine resonance between incarnations.

If we find ourselves upon an astral realm that we feel we have outgrown, we should rest assured that there is something within the permanent atoms of this plane that needs to find resolution. We will quickly move beyond this phase, as long as we remain open to the lessons that we are intended to learn. This is equally true upon the physical, although things move a bit slower down here. The more quickly we are willing to learn, the swifter we will move beyond the needed lessons and begin to function at a higher level.

Almost all serious students of the occult, whether or not they are familiar with its particular jargon, will find themselves on the higher levels of the astral and/or mental realms. The permanent atoms are our recording devices, which bear the records of our intent, motivations and actions and not the particular jargon or language we use to express this. If, however, a seemingly unexplained lesson comes our way, the best way to deal with it is by our greater understanding of the law of karma, a surrendering to the needed lesson and a willingness to make the necessary adjustments as quickly as possible to free ourselves to move beyond them. In psychology this is called acceptance. In Buddhism it is called nonresistance. In Hinduism, Sai Baba has referred to this as an attitude of welcoming adversity. This helps tremendously in experiencing any lesson, by letting go of attachment and surrendering to the process of God. I then proceed to ask God and the masters for their divine help and grace to move as quickly as possible through the needed lesson, so that nothing less than the purest energy of God is manifesting within my life. Know that no matter what you are dealing with, if you take but one step toward God and the masters, they will take ten steps toward you. It is important to understand, beloved readers, that you can request that God and the masters speed up the processing of your karma. On the other side of the coin, you can also make a similar request to slow it down if you are feeling overwhelmed by the lessons of life. Please bear this in mind, for God and the masters work with you in a cocreative partnership.

Devachan and the Buddhic Realms

When a soul has reached a high enough stage in its development, before reincarnating again into the material world, he/she is allowed to spend time within that lofty realm, which is the true dwelling place of the higher self or oversoul. This is a place of glorious bliss and divine perception, where from a state of beatitude one can look upon all the causes and effects (karma) of his many lifetimes. Along with one's higher self, guardian angel, the master(s) with whom he/she has been working and the Lords of Karma themselves, he decides upon the most appropriate way in which to work through and adjust that karma.

This is the God perspective of which I spoke earlier. While free temporarily from the influence of the permanent atoms of the physical/etheric, astral and mental bodies, one can look at his life patterns as whole and as the higher self, and thus participate in making the best possible choices for the future.

There comes an ultimate point within each initiation where we are freed from working through the lower worlds altogether. As this was stated earlier, I will not repeat the details here. The point I seek to make is that even though returning to the lower planes of manifestation, the experience of this higher realm gives us the needed perspective to work more diligently on our ascension process, having the perspective of the higher self and enjoying the blissful time within the high sphere where our cumulative progress has earned us the right of entry. This gift, and even greater ones, awaits every one of us who seek to live beyond the faulty belief of separateness and to dwell instead within the lofty regions of unity and oneness.

In considering our participation in the cleansing, clearing and purifying of our karma, the buddhic/devachan realm, a realm of pure bliss, must be brought into our awareness. If I were to leave out this higher perspective, which is truly the realm of the soul, then you might have the false impression that one can gain the needed understanding and wisdom to proceed through the astral and/or mental lens. This would then be a very limited understanding indeed. The part that our physical/etheric, astral and mental selves play is most significant, but the true understanding of these aspects can only be seen correctly from the perspective of the higher self and eventually the monadic self. As it is from the buddhic plane that we, as the higher self, are enabled to work from above downward and to cooperate consciously with the Lords of Karma, it seems fitting that I give you a close look into this realm.

I hope the brief peek into this higher perception has shed some light on it, though, in all likelihood, you are probably more familiar with this glorious realm than you might at first think. The essence of what I wish to impart to your conscious minds is that the more evolved one becomes upon the path of initiation and ascension, the more involved one becomes in its very process. This awareness will help you see that the trend of your life, the trend of all who are upon the conscious path of ascension/initiation, is one in which you/they as souls have sought to bring forth to make the most efficient progress.

Although you might still be working with the dynamics of the records of your permanent atoms, you are not simply victims of the past. Rather, you are cocreators of your destiny and have, with the aid of the Lords of Karma, created for yourself the situations that hold the best potential for your ultimate liberation and ascension. Beloved readers, take advantage of the moment and of every single opportunity for growth. Be aware that every cause has its effect and creates the most beneficial, spiritual and uplifting causes for yourself and the world, of which you and all of us are a divine part.

The Lords of Karma and Other
Karmic Overseers

Nothing happens by chance. The working of karma is quite an intricate process, bringing into play a multiplicity of unseen and subtle forces. There are, therefore, great spiritual beings whose divine job it is to help this law work out in the most efficient and productive way possible.

One of the main groups of beings is called the Lords of Karma. They guide and oversee the playing out of the continuous stream of deed and intent from humanity, interpenetrating physical/etheric, astral and mental bodies and worlds. It is interesting that the thought and thought/motivation of humanity will both individually and collectively outpicture upon the mental world that we find in any given incarnation. The same is true for the astral/emotional motivations and the purity with which any desire is brought into manifestation. The same holds true, as well, for the physical, which holds to the law that any physical good that is brought forth (no matter what the motive), will soon reap the reward on the physical world. It is important to keep in mind, however, that the good or positive physical karma can hold a severe emotional or mental lesson if the motive from past causes was self-serving.

There is also what is known in occult literature as the karmic board, which functions as the governing board of the Lords of Karma. It is set up as a review board where beings who have reached a certain high degree of initiation can on the inner planes come to speak, confer and file complaints or commendations. All is noted by the board, and no one should go lightly or casually before it. To do so also involves an act of karma upon the being who asks for a special hearing. If, however, you have deeply searched your heart about a given situation and your motives are pure, the great ones who comprise this board are available for consultation, as their entire jurisdiction lies within the realm of karma per se, and they are only too willing to be of service.

The recording angels are a group upon the angelic line of evolution who likewise work with the karma of individuals and collective wholes. The forces that determine the actual working out of karma upon the four lower bodies and in the four lower worlds take into account all that humanity does, desires and acts upon, as well as the interplay of astrological influences, ray influences and collective karma (which, for example, would draw a specific group of people into a so-called major accident or plane crash). These factors are so intricate that many spiritual beings hold office relating to this issue alone.

Reincarnation and Karma

As one might well imagine, the law of karma as played out from life to life involves an intricate pattern. This law, however, manifesting within the currents of cause and effect, is always just and fair, though often not apparently so. Let us look at the whole process, as best we are able, then break it down into specific instances that often leave humanity bereft, bewildered and lost in the agonies of seeming injustices.

As we discussed, the physical/etheric, astral and mental seed atoms contain the complete record of our past. During specific lifetimes, certain seeds are called forth to bear the fruit planted in previous lifetimes. This is referred to as *ripe karma*, for it is karma that is called forth from the vine upon which it was grown to bear the appropriate fruits within a given lifetime.

Let us say, for example, that during a certain lifetime or even a series of lifetimes, an individual was extremely cruel, dominating and unjust in his/her treatment of humanity. Perhaps he was, for example, an unfair ruler who sent people to dungeons, had them tortured, maimed and killed. This particular person would have built extreme negativity into his physical/etheric, astral and emotional permanent atoms, and the time will arrive when he must indeed pay the piper.

Having done such extreme injury to humanity on every level, this individual will have to face for himself the reality that he cruelly dispensed upon his brothers and sisters. In being born at the time when this karma is coming back on him, first appropriate parents will be selected who will have a specific tie to that individual and whose needs must face an interrelated karmic pattern. This infant, who is in truth an adult soul, might well be born disfigured and even mentally retarded. Now, lest anyone start to either judge or blame themselves for a given predicament, let me emphatically state two vital points: First, this is ultimately not a punishment but a lesson, so that the soul can break free of the limited view that resulted in past negative behavior; second, people born with similar difficulties are not necessarily born that way due to a similar cause. There might well be a highly advanced soul who chooses a similar incarnation to take upon him/herself the burden that a loved one might otherwise have to carry alone or for a variety of other reasons. Therefore, read this segment with absolutely no judgment, whatever your current situation might be.

From a place of total nonjudgment, then let us continue our example. This soul, born with difficulties on almost every level, might then be reflecting the physical, emotional and mental wounds he/she inflicted on others in the past. The parents might be others who participated in a similar type of behavior and who are given the chance to clear their karma by providing their child with loving care and kindness. The child will hope-fully learn what it feels like to have to struggle against such adversity and will never again (having experienced for himself what he forced others to experience) have anything to do with deliberately harming another human being.

Seen through the eyes of the personality only, such a family situation would likely be viewed as cruel, horrible and most assuredly unjust. Many times, such situations seem to offer proof that there is indeed no God at all. Actually, the reverse is just the case, and it is not God who created such suffering, but the law of karma—a tool given by God that humanity might grow into evolved, expanded and enlightened beings.

This information is from the point of view of the higher self, not that of the personality. Wonderful spiritual personages such as Edgar Cayce, Paramahansa Yogananda, Sai Baba and Babaji (who can see directly into the soul) have given specific accounts of why certain people have had to experience seemingly undue trials and tribulations. I share this with you because it is a truer, broader vision and will hopefully help you walk through your karmic situations with a degree of grace and surrendering that would not be possible if only looked at through a three-dimensional lens or the lens of the personality.

Remember, all that occurs is for our growth, betterment, ultimate cleansing and purification, so that we might all overcome our limitations, walking the Earth and traversing the heavens as God-realized ascended beings! I realize that there is so much apparent injustice in the world that it necessitates a true *seeing* via the higher self to really grasp the full truth of what I am saying. My request, therefore, is that you seek attunement so that you might better understand for yourselves the workings of this most mysterious law of karma.

One image you might find helpful in understanding the greater vision of karma is that of a jigsaw puzzle picturing a sky filled with resplendent stars and colorful planets. If you begin to piece together the puzzle and for the first few pieces pick up only the midnight-black sky, you might deduce that you are indeed putting together a very dark and bleak puzzle.

If, however, you stick with it, you very soon find all the silver, plati-num and gold stars and the colorful, multifaceted planets that constitute the bulk of the puzzle. The process of understanding karma is much the same. The first few pieces, (those that are presented to our outer vision) might appear dark and bleak. If, however, we have the staying power of true disciples and initiates of spirit, I assure you the puzzle that will un-fold before our inner vision will be so filled with brightness that it will take our inner eyes and hearts some time to grow accustomed to the glories we behold. Patience, perseverance, meditation, study, reading and self-inquiry are the keys, coupled with the willingness to be open to the wonderful destiny that awaits all who persevere on the pathway of light and love.

Group Karma

Group karma is a most interesting phenomenon. When certain karma becomes simultaneously ripe in a given group of individuals, members of this group are then drawn into a similar circumstance to work this karma out. This can range from being stuck in an elevator together or being hostages in a bank robbery to the horror of an airplane crash. This karma would ripen within the appropriate astrological cycle of the individuals, as well. The law is quite intricate.

There are no simple accidents, only the working out of karma. This, however, is a delicate point, because karma can work itself out through the vehicle of apparent accidents. The misjudging of certain technical functions on a given aircraft is a form of accidental oversight, to be sure, yet one that is then used by the Lords of Karma and the unconscious to work out karma within individuals who share this similar karma. Emotionally that is a very difficult concept to grasp; all we can ask is that you try to get a spiritual sense of what is being said.

The world is moving toward learning from grace rather than from karma. It is hoped that the more we all center ourselves in God, the less karma we will have to work out physically. We do this by clearing ourselves inwardly through prayer, meditation, invocation, affirmation, doing good deeds, learning from our own mistakes and the mistakes of others and clearing the negative ego. It is true that before this happens, karma is being accelerated as more souls request to heal all the cleavages within themselves through the quickest means possible, which often includes a combination of grace as well as a physical working out of karma. The main thing to remember is that God is ever on our side and wants us each to move into a state of purity and realization, unity and liberation, as quickly and in as whole and complete a manner as possible.

Impersonal Collective Karma

There are, however, karmic forces to which we find ourselves subjected that are not within our own permanent seed atoms or our own particular destiny, but are part of the destiny of the world as a whole. In cases of war, great planetary upheaval, and even murder in some instances, we are simply drawn into situations that are much bigger than each of us individually. If caught in these situations, we can choose to use them to further cleanse and purify ourselves or our loved ones by offering that karmic suffering up to God. Just by being part of humanity, it is not unusual to find ourselves involved in some karmic drama that we ourselves have not called forth.

In the extreme cases of murder, it has been said by spiritual teachers and channelers that murder victims are often paying off a karmic debt called forth from their ripe karma. There are, however, many cases where murder actually interferes with the karmic purpose of individuals who find themselves caught in a sort of collective world madness, with the result that they experience truly wrongful deaths. This is a bitter pill to swallow. However, rest assured that in being caught in the crossfire of this type of karma or that of war, famine, plague, earthquake, flood and so forth, much karma that would have otherwise been slowly and less dramatically worked through is instantly wiped away, and that soul is cleared in a moment's time of what would have extended over lifetimes.

This is, most assuredly, not to say there is anything *right* in this. It is to say that the laws of God will and do make it right, and no one is left to suffer without being carefully watched over, tended to and ultimately healed.

The concept of collective and impersonal karma might be a new one to many long-term students of the occult, but it is worth considering. We are, after all, part of humanity and sometimes subjected to trends and karma that are the movement of the greater outpicturing of the eddies, tides, currents and crosscurrents of the world we inhabit. This is yet another reason, my beloved readers, to lay all judgments aside.

On a more individual note, the blind person you see stumbling through the darkness might be the saint who chooses a lifetime to focus on the inner light only and is not, as in an example Edgar Cayce gave, the karmic result of one who blinded another in a previous life. The one point I would like you to take to heart in this discussion of karma is, they who have the ability to truly see, judge not. And they who do not know often judge, and judge in error. Therefore, observe, learn, but never, ever judge.

How then do we, moving through this sea of karma, live our lives? The answer is quite simply, to the best of our ability and with constant attunement to the oneness that joins us with God, and therefore with the stream of the whole of life. Truly, karma is best understood through the intuition and the higher self, because all occult wisdom is a subject ultimately brought to light within each person's own heart as he/she moves forward upon the path of integrated ascension. Love, wisdom and service to others is the great eraser of karma, and it lies within each of our grasps to claim and manifest every moment of our lives. The true power of transmutation and healing ultimately lies with each one of us. Let us never forget that all karma is a gift from God, if we will just look at it as God would have us see it.

6

Opening to the Higher Senses
Experiences
on the Path of Ascension

Although it is possible that you are new to the understanding of many concepts in this book, it is equally possible that you are familiar with some of the common sensations and experiences that accompany the initiatory and ascension process. This is more than likely, since those of you reading this book are probably initiates of one degree or another. It might not have been brought through to your conscious awareness until now, however, for many of these initiations take place while you sleep. The basic truth is that all of us on this path at some point begin to receive stimulations, impressions and responses of sensitivity that might at first be unexpected and unfamiliar. In this chapter I will explain some basic sensations, as well as the more refined ones, to help eliminate confusion you might have and explain what you are, in fact, experiencing.

Sensing Unity with All Things

One of the first feelings we experience as we enter the path of initiation is the sensing of unity or oneness with all humanity and, indeed, with all things. There is usually a feeling of abundant love and joy that seems to permeate all people, animals, plant life, every form and manifestation upon the Earth, extending to the heavens themselves. This might at first take the newly awakening initiate by surprise, yet there is usually a feeling of familiarity that accompanies these feelings, along with the sensation of great peace, love and desire to be of service.

This feeling occurs from the dawn of the initiatory process and at certain stages along the path of probation because we are sensing the truth of that to which we are all connected. The real surprise would be if we did not experience these feelings at all, since what is happening is a tuning in to the deeper and fuller nature of our selves. To some people, based on their particular disposition and attunement, these sensations of oneness flow through the heart in great expansive waves of love. For others it is a much more subtle recognition. Therefore, do not seek to measure your progress, now or ever, against another person's experiences. Do, however, be aware that these types of feelings are quite natural and allow yourself to experience them without any sense of confusion or fear.

The wonderful feelings of oneness will ultimately grow and expand with each succeeding initiation, as you grow more in touch with your higher self, monad, God and the masters. The path of initiation and ascension brings one into the ever-more inclusive whole, and likewise it brings forth into the conscious awareness the sensing of these realms of unity. Be prepared, therefore, for greater and greater feelings of love and light, peace and unity to enfold you in the aura of your true divine nature.

Out of this knowingness of being one with the One does the opening of the higher senses and sensings occur. For what is happening is that you are expanding into that all-inclusive and embracing aspect of self. The energies from the higher realms, from the masters and from God cannot help but flood your four lower bodies with the light from above or light from within. The paradox remains that the planes, or realms, and bodies are of a higher frequency than are those of the dense material world, yet they interpenetrate the material world and each other.

As the process of ascension unfolds, you can be sure that more and more will be revealed from these higher sources. It is a most wondrous divine adventure we are on! Keep always in the fore of your minds that each persons' path is unique unto itself, veritably spun as a spider spins its web—out of the very substance of its own being. There is one joint rule that all must follow: Do not compare, compete or judge yourselves based on the unfoldments of others. This is important, for we each have our own puzzle piece to fulfill, and no two are exactly alike. If they were, God would not have bothered with the process of individualization in the first place, but would have made only one aspect of self. Although one, we are indeed many and therein, my beloved readers, lies the beauty of it all. The phrase, "unity in diversity," speaks to this truth.

As Paramahansa Yogananda eloquently said, "the path to God is not a circus." I believe he said this so that his disciples would not get caught up in some of the particular phenomena I will now address. Also I think he said this to help his disciples steer clear of comparisons and jealousies as to who among them had gone further along the path via this or that ability or vision. His statement serves to reiterate my point that the path is an individualized one, and that, although I feel it's very necessary to look at the higher senses and developments we will go through along the way, that we do this in the clear light of understanding, not the muddy light of petty comparisons.

The Development of Intuition

In the development of intuition there are two distinct phases and aspects through which it manifests. The first is instinctual and involves the solar plexus, or third-chakra area. This is demonstrated when a parent senses that his/her child is in danger, or conversely, the child senses that a parent has fallen ill or crossed over. This is related also to the more emotional aspect of self, and it can occur any time in a person's development.

The higher aspect is the development of the intuitive mind, which is linked to the causal/buddhic, or fourth realm and body. In these instances you begin to get clear impressions from the higher self, and the higher qualities of intuition are brought forth.

From the higher intuition we begin to see things as they are, piercing the veil of simply reasoning from the conscious mind or feeling from the lower emotional body. We are put in touch with a greater sensing and can therefore bring into our consciousness the higher knowing. Examples are when, through intuition, we get a true and clear sense of where a person is coming from. We do not simply hear with our ears, but are able to intuit the intent and motivation behind the words. This serves us well in being able to get an accurate "read" on a person, and it is extremely helpful in the event we are asked to trust him/her in spiritual, personal or professional capacities. This would extend into business contacts, as well. We must no longer rely only upon our ability to read between the lines, but also upon our ability to almost instantaneously intuit the ultimate motives of an individual.

This is especially helpful in healing or counseling work. When we enter into the field of the healing arts, no matter what our particular form of healing or the methods, it is extremely important that we have a well-developed intuition to be of the greatest possible service. The more we advance on the path, the easier it will become to intuit the world around us, as well as seeing through the outer layers of people and situations. My advice would be to request from God, your higher self and the masters an increase of intuition in your chosen path of service to greater facilitate your work. The masters are anxious to help those who seek to help the whole through service, and requesting help will definitely bring the needed response.

Realize that God and the masters help those who seek to help the God-self within others, and are therefore only too eager to aid the process of one part helping self and serving another part of self. This is an interpretation based on the lens of the unity of all life—one of which I am very fond.

It is also through higher intuition that we come to *know* the higher aspects of truth. That which seems to defy the logically reasoning mind can be grasped easily by the intuition. Besides the subconscious and conscious mind, there is the superconscious or higher mind, which is an aspect of intuition. It is by this mind of intuition that we sense the reality of all the masters. And with that more abstract part of ourselves, we know and sense the truth of these deeper aspects of beingness.

At later stages on the path of initiation it becomes possible to intuit what level of intuition we have achieved. We must, however, make sure that the negative-ego mind is not doing the seeing for us, and thus either raising us to a higher level of initiation than that which we have actually reached (out of its own desire to be at that place) or lowering us to a less advanced stage because some part of ourselves does not think we have come as far along as we actually have.

This theme of keeping the negative ego out of the way is aptly applied to all areas that involve using our intuition. Therefore, it becomes important to set the intent of getting the negative-ego mind out of the way so that we may more clearly know truth as it is through the higher knowing of intuition.

Intuition's Place in Dreams

As we proceed along the ascension path, it is common to have more spiritual dreams. These dreams are not coming from the subconscious-mind function of working things out via dreams, nor are they simply dreams of retelling the day's events so we can process these happenings. However, working with these nonspiritual dreams can reveal much that is going on with us and can greatly help our psychological understanding.

The dreams that come through the higher intuitive sense are often the actual recounting of inner-plane spiritual encounters. These encounters may come through clearly or symbolically, and they are of a higher nature. People often recall attending classes of occult studies on the inner realms that are held at intervals by the masters. There might be dreams of precognition that prepare us for events of a personal or planetary nature with which we will be involved. There might be dreams of actual encounters with specific masters on the inner plane where the conversations might or might not be recollected by the conscious mind, but the knowingness of the meeting with the master is brought forth in total clarity.

When dealing with dreams of this nature, it is up to the individual to discern for him/herself just how accurate the dream is with regard to intuition. It often takes skill and practice to be able to distinguish the subconscious dream from the superconscious one. But, in time, this will come. In the meantime, writing down your dreams can be of enormous value because you will then learn to understand both what the subconscious mind and the superconscious mind/higher intuition are trying to tell you, as well as from which place within the dream is truly originating.

Developing Psychic Abilities

Psychic development functions much the same as intuitive development in that there is both a lower and higher form. The lower form centers on personality issues only and relates primarily to the four lower bodies. It generally comes from the negative-ego consciousness rather than the Christ consciousness. It might come also from subconscious desires, of which the personality is not even aware. In essence, this means that it comes from a place the lower self taps into and then proceeds to interpret, or the subconscious desire is revealed to the psychic reader and that is what is inevitably addressed rather than the truth of things. Usually the advice offered by such a psychic can, at best, give only half-formed images pertaining solely to the personality aspect of his/her client, who then interprets it through only the lower and incomplete lens of the personality. Or it might come entirely from the negative ego's faulty belief system. However, lower-form psychics have been of genuine service to humanity by helping police locate missing children and so forth.

But at its worst, this lower form of psychic function can create self-fulfilling prophecies of a negative nature; for instance, when a psychic says he/she foresees illness, loss or death in a vulnerable client's life. This client is then prone to bringing that forth to one degree or another through the power of this negative imagery created by the psychic. Initiates and disciples are therefore guided to avoid consultations with psychics functioning at this level for their own spiritual, mental, emotional and physical well-being. They are usually easy to spot, for they deal exclusively with the lower levels of the personality and are definitely, if subtly, manipulative, often portraying themselves as having all the answers. Rather than encourage clients to access their own guidance by contacting their higher selves or intuition and use the advice given as helpful insights to be worked with, they instead present their clairvoyance as immutable laws, which render the client powerless. If you sense this attitude when seeking communion with the inner realms, run for the hills! For all you will receive from these psychics are loosely garbled images they are picking up from the lower spheres in an attempt to feed their negative egos and hold a position of power. Forget these spirit guides from the astral/mental planes and move on to a high-grade spiritualized psychic and/or channeler of spirit and the ascended masters.

The higher psychic really works from higher intuition, with the aid of his/her higher self, God and the masters. This psychic also often has channeling ability, which will be discussed at length in this chapter. For now, please bear in mind that the channel, higher telepath or spiritual counselor deals very little with the personality, except how best to use the lessons that the client is dealing with to further his/her process of initiation and ascension. The higher psychic does not work out of the negative ego, but rather out of the christed mind and higher self/monad, seeking only to be of service to the client or friend on all possible levels.

They usually work under the guidance of one or more inner-plane masters to quickly and clearly get to the heart of the matter. Functioning from above downward, the greater vision is theirs, and it is this they seek to impart.

These higher psychics with channeling abilities have a purity of motive and do not seek to control anyone. Their only aim is to help guide you in the highest possible direction upon your path and to learn from the realms of perception to which they have access. They operate out of the inner knowing of the higher intuition, with no motives other than to be of service. Many of you who are now awakening to these higher aspects of self will find the psychic centers likewise opening within you. Use your own discretion as you open up to make sure the impressions that you receive are coming from the highest possible aspect of self that you can access.

It is important that you check to be sure that you are not acting out of the negative ego or lower self, but rather out of the Christ consciousness and/or higher self and monad. This is not as complicated as it might sound. Simply ask your higher self, in the name of Christ or any one of the inner-plane masters with whom you work, as well as God, whether you are functioning and receiving information from the highest level of yourself or not. God will not lie to you, nor will the masters. The only trick is in making sure that you do not block the clear answer that you are intended to receive by allowing the personality aspect of self to interfere.

This simple formula will refine your intuition and bring you into full rapport with the highest aspects of self. Add to it the ingredient of asking to be placed in a protected aura of divine light and love from the onset of your attunement process. Tell God, the masters and your higher self that you want to receive only psychic impressions that will be of service to humanity's process of evolution, as well as your own. Include that you want to function only from your spiritual or Christ mind and that any influence from the negative ego or astral and mental planes be dissipated.

Developing these qualities is a gift from God. When rightly used from the purest place and in the service of humanity you are returning the gift to God with the richness that you are bringing into your work. Do not be afraid of these higher qualities and abilities within you. They come as a natural part of your ascension process. Do be sure, however, they are kept aligned with the spiritual mind and not the negative ego. Also, beloved readers, as with all other abilities of a spiritual nature, ever bear in mind that no two people develop the exact same qualities and certainly not to the same degree. Stick to your own destiny and divine puzzle piece. Remember, you are the path, and in joy proceed to work with the path and light you are.

Channeling and Higher Telepathy

One interesting phenomenon of our present time is the emergence of the channeler. People in great numbers are now able to make contact with the higher levels of self, monad, God and the masters and to bring through, to varying degrees of clarity, information from the higher realms. This really is not something new, for it has existed throughout the ages. Beings who had evolved were always able to go within and hear the voices therein.

This was often referred to as "the still small voice within," where humanity was guided to go to make contact with God. The basic conscious channeler of today's world would, in fact, have been the prophet of old. The great difference between then and now is the fact that humankind as a whole is traversing the higher realms through an accelerated process, and what was once available only to the chosen few is now available to increasing numbers of people.

From another vantage point, we are and have always been channeling information/feelings from the four lower bodies, the subconscious mind and the world in which we live. We bring through images and feelings that have affected us from these sources and interpret them as truth. However, here we are looking at the channeler who is an awakening initiate attempting to contact or in contact with realms of intuition and masters. This is being mastered more as we evolve. Some basic challenges are those intrinsic to developing of psychic abilities and intuition. There are many areas where channeling dovetails into these other areas. One such area to be mindful of in developing your channeling and other psychic abilities is to watch over the negative ego's interference, as well as to be as clear as possible that the information you are receiving is indeed coming from the higher realms and not from your own lower self or personality levels. As with other professions, there is a certain percentage among psychics/channelers that could be classified as charlatans—unscrupulous individuals who exploit people's trust for financial gain. One must be mindful of these out-to-make-a-fast-buck types. The best way to separate the wheat from the chaff is to ask the masters for guidance and to trust your own intuition, as well. Fortunately, these fraudulent practitioners tend to be more the exception than the rule. But, even among the genuine articles, there is some variation in quality.

There is no judgment when I say that some channelers or higher spiritual telepaths are clearer than others. It is simply a statement of fact based
on discernment. The clearer the channel is in regard to his/her own psychological issues, the more he is centered in the higher self/monad and
can get the personality out of the way, bringing through clearer information. Understand that all channelers, even the best on the planet, are
bringing information through their personal information banks and belief
systems. The guidance here is to take advantage of external channels, but
always take the information with a grain of salt and, again, trust your own
intuition and inner guidance above all else. This is why I emphasize the
importance of clearing the negative ego's way of thinking and rising to the
Christ level of thinking. This puts one in rapport with the spiritual aspect
of self and brings to a minimum any interference by the lower aspects of
self.

This brings us into subtler but extremely vital realms. Because people
are passing through their initiations at greater speeds due to the acceleration of the planet as a whole and the rapid raising of the light quotient, the
higher planes are becoming much more easily accessible to us. The point
must be driven home, however, that hand in hand with this wonderful acceleration of the initiation process must come the development of psychological awareness through opening the heart center and a willingness to
overcome the lower tendencies that allow negative-ego thinking and
lower-self desire in even some of the most advanced initiates.

I keep drawing this to your attention, beloved readers, because especially if you are a beginner, the more integrated your approach to the process of initiation is, the better you will fare in the long run. I also bring this
to your attention so that when you seek out channelers, spiritual counselors or spiritual groups with which to support you in your own work, you
will be sure that they are of the highest standing.

There is a familiar saying, "blinded by the light," and this is just what
I seek to prevent happening to you through your own unintegrated development or through allowing anyone else (including the authors of this
book) to tell you what to do. The purpose of my books is to guide and enlighten and that should be the only acceptable purpose motivating any to
whom you go for help and support along the way. I don't mind repeating
myself in cautioning you against anyone, no matter how high he/she claims
to be or what powers he possesses, who uses any form of personal manipulation over you. This is simply not to be tolerated. There are far too many
pure channels, spiritual counselors and healers in the world to settle for
anything less than those who seek to aid you from the clearest, highest and
purest place possible. Remember, you are ultimately your own master,
higher self and monad, who is one with God. You are on the path of

discovering the heights and depths of this oneness, but it is *your* path. Any true channeler or spiritual counselor will honor that and seek only to work with you in developing your own point of connection and your own clarity. Therefore, I repeat, if anyone seeks to manipulate, dominate, control or instill fear in you, just walk away.

Having said all that, I will proceed with discussing the more positive aspects of channeling, spiritual counseling and higher telepathy. As we grow into our higher bodies, we begin to resonate with greater frequencies of light and love, which puts us in touch with the inner-plane ascended beings, the planetary and (on higher levels) cosmic hierarchies. The wisdom and radiance of their higher and clearer knowing is then able to find a place of resonance within our own elevated four-body system and through the development of our higher intuitive powers. We are then in rapport with them and gain access to wisdom they can offer to be of greater service to our own ascension process.

We likewise become, in ever-greater degrees, more connected with our own higher selves. These higher aspects are likewise able to impart a vast amount of wisdom to our minds, as well as to run currents of healing, devotional, revelatory and accelerating energies through our four-body systems.

Accessing both our higher selves and monads, we then become conscious channelers of this wisdom, love and healing energy. We gain the ability to work in this manner with both our own spiritual aspects and those of the inner-plane masters of the Hierarchy. As I said before, the clearer we are with self, the clearer channels we will be. We must understand that every initiate will channel differently. Some will channel clairaudiently through speaking, others telepathically through thought, while others energetically through art, music, poetry, dance and love.

Individuals are chosen by certain masters because of their particular personality type to bring through higher energies in a way specific only to them. For example, the master Paul the Venetian, working on the fourth ray or energy frequency of the arts, will likely search out someone with an artistic nature to best express the higher truths. Sometimes masters will work with one another, and an initiate will have the blending of Paul the Venetian's artistic nature with the master Djwhal Khul's great cosmic wisdom, manifesting in poetry or song. Many of the arts throughout history were produced through the joint energy flow of the creative or fourth-ray energies and the devotional energy of Jesus or the sixth-ray, which can be seen in the religious art of Rome and Florence, Italy.

Along these same lines, masters blend with those who express certain qualities. This means that not only does a person color the messages he/she brings through by virtue of his own personal nature, but for the very reason he is chosen to channel that energy. Here is another reason to keep purifying the psychological system. We want to be as available as possible to help manifest the work of the Spiritual Hierarchy upon Earth and the more pure, clear and right with self we are, the more able we will be to do this. Many channels and psychics think they are clear, but in truth they are not. This is a lesson of spiritual discernment for the rapidly developing initiate. Just because a person channels something, doesn't make it true. Many spiritual teachers speak from their own mastery and don't clairaudiently voice channel, yet their information and godliness is far more refined, pure and from a higher source than those channeling.

In looking for a channel or spiritual counselor with whom to work, you will probably be most comfortable with one who shares your own or similar attunement and spiritual path. Also, when you work in this manner (as you will to some degree simply by virtue of your own attunement to your higher self, monad and the masters), do not expect your own communications to have nothing of yourself in them. You must continually invoke the clearest, highest and purest communication possible, allowing the higher self and the masters to express truth without the distortions of negative-ego faulty thinking or the misguidance of your own personal agenda taking over.

By now you can see that there is a fine line between the interference of the personality and using the personality to bring forth wisdom. Although the line between the two is thin, it is ironclad and it is each individual's responsibility to remain on one side of the line or the other. If we are honest with self and keep our attention focused on God and truth, then the help and guidance the inner-plane masters have to impart will be of unparalleled value.

The Call to Channel

It is important to say that channeling or being a spiritual telepathic counselor or teacher will not be everyone's calling. Some might work as spiritual counselors and therefore receive direct guidance from the masters to serve their students, clients, friends and the world at large. Some initiates, however, might bring through the energies of the masters and higher realms strictly through vibration and work through the radiance of their energy fields. Such people range from householders to business people. They will not necessarily be conscious channels and yet, guided by the voice of their higher intuitive selves, will live in total harmony with divine intent. These individuals will have as close a connection to the masters as the channeler, but they will be working out of an inner sensing rather than a conscious communion with the masters themselves. Their own work could likewise change the world and hasten the manifestation of the plan of God on Earth.

People in the political, business, householder, mechanical, construction, technical and other arenas hold as valuable positions as do those who are in the roles of conscious channelers and spiritual teachers. There are many walks in life, and this is by divine design. There are seven different rays, or energy streams, operating within the sphere of our Earth, solar system and the cosmos, and each of these rays is responsible for calling into manifestation various aspects of being through which humanity finds expression. The wonderful thing about the science of the rays is that it incorporates and synthesizes the myriad of pathways taken by humanity, validating that each has its appropriate place in the scheme of things. One, therefore, does not have to follow a religious or telepathic path to be working in cooperation with the divine plan. Again, to each his/her appropriate puzzle piece, and unto each his/her own unique connection to God.

Energy Rushes

There is a great movement of energy when one is quickly accelerating the initiatory process, which is due to a variety of factors. One is a shifting polarization from one body to another and from one frequency within a particular body to a higher frequency, or rate of vibration.

For example, if you generally react from the dominating needs of the physical and desire/astral body and have shifted your polarization to the mental body, where you now focus your attention on controlling the lower impulses of lust and over-emotionalism, then you are shifting polarization from the physical and emotional bodies to the next one above. On the other hand, if you are raising your emotional body from a depressive self-pitying mode, or a mode of conditional love, into a state of divine joy and unconditional love, then you are shifting polarization within the same body.

During the path of initiation and ascension, both shiftings take place simultaneously. The rate of vibrational frequency and resonance within each of the bodies goes through a process of spiritualization and energy shift. Likewise the focus of attention shifts from the lower four bodies into the bodies that constitute the higher self and ultimately, the monadic self. One does not forget about the lower bodies, which is something many initiates need to realize. Each body we live in has a definite purpose. The goal is to have each of these bodies functioning at the highest possible frequency to bring through at any given time the impulses and guidance of the higher bodies. The goal, therefore, is the integration of the four lower bodies with those of the higher to create one divinely functioning whole.

From the point where changing frequencies is great enough to make a true impact upon the bodies, all the way through the ascension initiation and beyond, one becomes subject to certain energy rushes. This is the outward feeling of the inner process of moving energy both within the bodies and from body to body. This might result also from contact with one or several masters or one's higher self and monad.

Often this movement of energy actually feels like a rush of pure energy through the four-body system. Or you might find yourself feeling lighthearted (which, indeed, accurately describes the infusion of light within the head region). You might feel a tingling sensation along the spine or on top of the head, signifying contact with the soul/monad or one of the masters. I have come to know that I am in contact with certain masters based upon a particular pattern of tingling sensations that occur along my spine and on the top of my head. These energy patterns are interesting to watch and pleasurable, I might add. And once you are aware of them, they become familiar friends.

I would be remiss, however, if I did not point out that some energy shifts can be a bit uncomfortable. Often when the third-eye area is becoming awakened, headaches will be experienced due to the increase in stimulation. Sometimes the lightheadedness can be less than comfortable. The thing to remember is that even as this is occurring, there is an inner-plane team of healers always available to help you through the oddities that can occur as a result of the changing patterns of energy within you.

Tiredness might also occur, usually after a profound period of meditation or study. When you are tired, do make the time to get the rest you feel you require. This is a wonderful time to ask the inner-plane team of healers to help balance and adjust the energies within your four lower bodies, so that you may function more comfortably within them.

There is a specific master healer by the name of Dr. Lorphan (pronounced *Lor-pan*), who is available to all who call on him. He works with a team of spiritual healers and is adept at solving any difficulties that you might be having. Jesus/Sananda is a master healer, as is Lord Maitreya/Christ, and you are encouraged to call upon them if that feels more comfortable. The avatar Sai Baba is likewise a divine healer, and if you feel more attuned to him, then by all means call upon him. There is no end to the miracles that Sai Baba, as well as the other healers, can perform. You are not limited to the masters I have named, for there are several other wonderful master healers, including certain of the healing angels, who are there for the asking. I'm simply offering a few suggestions based upon some of the beings with whom I work. If you resonate with the following names, you might try calling on Melchizedek, Lord Metatron and the Mahatma, whose energy fields are incredible. For more comprehensive information on all the different planetary and cosmic masters, consider reading *The Complete Ascension Manual.*

It is an interesting path we are on, producing quite an array of vibrational shifts. Sometimes these energy rushes do not affect the purely physical vehicle at all, such as when you find yourself suddenly engulfed in a feeling of the most wonderful divine love. This is much more likely to affect the etheric heart chakra than the actual physical heart, and it can wash over you like a continuous wave of divine nectar.

This feeling of pure unconditional love is one of the most glorious sensations one can experience on the path of ascension. What is happening actually is that the heart chakra (located in etheric matter directly opposite the physical heart) begins to expand and expand and expand. This can occur as the direct result of one's own personal progress on the path of initiation. It also can be brought about through direct stimulation by one of the masters. These feelings cannot help but put you in touch with the unity of all life. You most likely will be in contact with the causal, or buddhic vehicle, your higher self and possibly your monad as well. In any event, the energy of divine love will both raise you up to one of your spiritual bodies and raise the vibrational frequencies within your four lower bodies through the heart chakra. This experience can only be described as pure grace.

Sensing a Master

Often upon the path of initiation/ascension you will have the experience of sensing the master's presence. This can occur either out of the blue or during meditation. The master(s) with whom you are working is often about you, helping you with your spiritual journey. As the various centers within you begin to awaken, it is common to have an overwhelming sense of the master as you move through the initiations and as the blend between your and the master's auras deepen. Sometimes you might experience the presence of your guardian angel, a common event since we all do have a guardian angel, a being who is upon the angelic line of evolution that runs parallel to the human line of evolution. There are spiritual masters and angels about us all the time, and therefore sensing their presence should not be surprising.

Hearing a Master

Some of us will actually hear the voice of the master, which is called clairaudience. It's much rarer in occurrence than is the inner hearing but it does occur nonetheless. Most hear the "still small voice within," and this is no less valid. But it is a strictly telepathic method since it involves communication through thought transference rather than the actual hearing mechanism.

Seeing a Master

Some people actually develop the ability to physically see the master, as well as the world of spiritual beings, including the angels. This is known as clairvoyance. What actually occurs in these cases is one of a few possibilities.

In some cases, the third eye of the initiate becomes so developed that it is able to easily pierce the veils between the physical worlds and see into the spiritual worlds. The consciousness in these situations is centered in the third eye and head area, so that the impressions received are coming from the causal/buddhic realms and those above it. If the seeing is being transmitted by the master from the etheric realm, know that the master has created a body by manipulating matter through spiritualized will. And masters have done so on the etheric realm to make specific contact with their students. In rare but proven cases masters create a dense enough vehicle to be perceived and made manifest upon the actual physical plane. This was done by the master Saint Germain when he contacted Guy Ballard (Godfre Ray King) on Mount Shasta to initiate the "I AM" movement and to have a series of books written under his tutelage. This was also done by El Morya, Kuthumi and Djwhal Khul during the theosophical movement in the nineteenth and early twentieth centuries.

One common place where you might see a master is within the inner planes during sleep. The master might choose this time to appear directly to you to impart either a specific teaching or to grant you *darshan*, an eastern religious term meaning the giving of grace and blessing. One might also learn how to bring through into waking consciousness full and total recollection of inner-plane experiences at seminars, which are a regular program of study for the initiate.

One might also see the master and the great host of spiritual beings, including the angels and archangels themselves. This was not uncommon throughout the ages in the case of artists, whose work portraying these beings can attest to the phenomenon. Specific masters and archangels are now in process of revealing themselves to many initiates all over the globe. The veil of separation between the inner-plane ascended masters and initiates on Earth has never been thinner than it is at this time.

The Sense of Pre-Vision

The gift of pre-vision has much to do with a person's ability to see simultaneously via the causal body both the cause and effect of any given situation. This is actually a relatively simple matter, since for every cause that is set in motion, there is the appropriate effect.

Since as human beings with free will the choice is always ours, we will have inevitably throughout time made decisions that were not of the highest nature and will hold within them a particular consequence, or karmic response. By virtue of being granted the pre-vision as to how a certain event will play itself out, we are given the chance to alter that effect by nullifying the karma that has brought it into being. This is one possible gift resulting from our initiatory process.

If one is granted the pre-vision of a certain accident occurring, one would likewise be shown the karma that brought it into being. The simultaneous seeing of both cause and effect will allow the initiate to offset that karma by expressing the opposite of that which was to set this in motion. This can be done through prayer, a change in attitude and a readjustment of action. The vision, in such a case, would be offered out of grace so that we may set things right and thus avert the otherwise predictable outplay of that karma.

On a broader scale, this is happening with many predictions regarding the fate of humanity and Earth herself. Certain great ones—prophets from biblical times, the Hopi Indians and more recently, those who have had visions of humanity's destiny if it continues its negative course of behavior—made some pretty dire predictions regarding the Earth's evolution (or more aptly put, her almost total destruction). What was seen or sensed was the *potentiality* of these events if the body of lightworkers and those attuned to the greatest good did not change the course and destiny to which humanity was heading—through prayer, transformation, love, meditation, inner communion, a willingness to learn from grace instead of karma and attitudinal healing. Dear reader, take heart, for this has indeed been accomplished.

The various spiritual groups dedicated to enlightenment and the upliftment of spirit within man—the healing groups, centers and activations across the globe, various prayer groups, the ascension movement, the willingness of humanity to respond to the call of the Hierarchy—all of these have collectively averted the predicted disasters. That this portion of humanity when compared to the masses is relatively small makes little difference at this level, for the needed work has been done. Set in motion by the body of lightworkers, it will then be gradually picked up by the masses of humanity in general. Great and significant progress was indeed made.

Now, I ask you to bear in mind that certain effects and eventualities will play themselves out, but to a much-reduced degree. There are two things we must remember.

First, certain adjustments need to be made by the very elevation of Earth itself. Just as there are energy rushes that occur to an individual while passing through the various stages of the initiation process, so too will Earth herself go through her own energy rushes. These will manifest as she seeks to readjust herself to the new vibrational frequencies within which she is now beginning to function. Therefore, there will still be certain Earth changes and shifts, but to such a reduced degree that it is almost impossible to relate the old vision to the new. This is intrinsic to the evolution of Earth herself.

Second, there likewise remains some negative forces still at play. These forces need a bit of a shaking up to shift from the negative-ego belief system and the ensuing destruction to an elevated system in which the four lower bodies of a certain mass of humanity are brought into enlightenment. Therefore, there will be some earth shifts, but nothing like the predictions of doomsday in prophetic texts such as those of Nostradamus and the biblical prophecies of Armageddon.

Now people need to stop picturing these predictions within their own minds and instead create visualizations of the manifestation of a golden era of civilization. The truth about prophecy is that prophecy is given forth so that it may be changed. With regard to the dire prophecies for planet Earth, this has certainly been the case. What must become a steady practice now is holding the most positive thought forms for ushering in the new millennium; understanding that so-called earth disturbances are due to raising frequencies; ever keeping your minds and hearts steady in light and love; being a part of the solution for planet Earth by focusing on the path of ascension (which includes clearing and cleansing negative-ego thought processes and replacing them by Christ-thinking); having daily contact with the masters and your higher self through meditation, prayer and the invocation of increased light and love; and anchoring your four lower bodies. Whenever possible, and that should be always, demonstrate the will-to-good through loving service to humanity and to yourselves, and keep ever mindful that you are and ever have been one with the One. By following these practices, both your personal and planetary karma will be lifted into the light. You, beloved readers, will learn how to learn from grace rather than from the effects of accumulated negative karma.

The vision of the future for self, friends and the world at large is given so that we may avert any collisions stemming from the past wrong misuse of the power of free will. If karma does come into our lives with a gentle nudge or a bang, let us learn the needed lesson and move on. One wonderful way of nullifying negative karma is not to react to it. This quiets storms, both figuratively and literally. Precognitive visions are a sign from God that grace has come our way and that by centering in our higher selves, God, the masters, light and love, the negative karma will be nullified by this divine alignment. In cases where it is not totally nullified, we must learn from it and know that the vision was shown to us so we will know from whence the karma came and can adjust all future actions accordingly. Remember, God is on our side, and all divine gifts, whatever their nature, are meant to speed us along the pathways of our divine destinies in as gentle and loving a way as possible.

Conclusion

As one evolves upon the path of initiation or ascension, there invariably follows the opening of the higher faculties of perception. This will occur differently and to varying degrees within each individual, as every person's path is unique. Although the higher faculties indicate a higher level of unfoldment, they by no means are the earmark of the initiate. For some, these particular qualities will have nothing to do with God's plan for them or their specific divine puzzle piece.

Likewise, be mindful that the realm of lower psychism should be avoided altogether. This might manifest in the calling forth of certain low-grade astral beings and asking them for guidance. Just because one has crossed over to the other side does not make him/her any more enlightened than he was on Earth. In fact, the case is most probably that if you are an initiate of even the earlier stages, you possess a greater knowingness than the mass of humanity available for contact on the other side.

I am not referring to linking up with a beloved on the other side of the veil, but rather to employing the indiscriminate use of the lower psychic centers to satisfy idle curiosity. This is quite dangerous and must definitely be guarded against. Never simply open yourself up to anyone who wants to come within your auric field. Always set the divine intent, along with a prayer request, that only the highest beings be allowed to make their impressions upon you. This is simple to understand if you but think of your auric field as your home. You likely do not keep your door at home wide open with a sign offering welcome to anyone who desires entry. All that I am really asking you to do is to protect yourselves psychically. Of course, you may ask the masters to help you contact a beloved mate or family member who has passed on. They will often grant this request to their disciples, and the joy and faith of such a request answered lifts one from the realm of grief and despair into utter joy and faith, and the knowledge of life eternal.

I have been extremely fortunate in this way myself. There was a person who passed on with whom my bond of love and connection ran so deep that words fail. This person passed on in another part of the country without my knowing about it on any conscious level and the passing was unexpected. We did, however, make a pact to know each other for who we are in the next life. Well, by the grace of God and the masters, I did not have to wait that long.

One morning, soon after his passing, I was relaxing when suddenly I felt his presence overlight and enter me. We literally roared in laughter—both he and I occupying the same body. It was like something out of Star Trek, where there were literally two essences, his and mine, occupying the same mind. After about a minute of this I left my body and looked down on *him*. I literally saw him there, laughing in love, joy and freedom, while I happily floated above in my etheric body. After a minute this passed. I was blown away and wanted to call him, but the day went as days go and soon two weeks had elapsed. After that I heard that my beloved friend had passed on shortly before our encounter.

Since this information did not come from someone I particularly trusted, I decided to ask God and my friend if this was true. I do not exaggerate when I tell you a photo of him literally floated into my hands. I was convinced. And a few subsequent phone calls confirmed this to be fact. Now, I cannot say that all the pain of the news of his physical passing was instantly transmuted; the emotions most definitely did their thing. However, as time has passed, the pain has given way to unparalleled divine joy and a knowingness that far supersedes faith itself—that love is eternal, and that within the cosmos of God, nothing of value is ever truly lost. I offer you this little story both as an inspiration and a tribute to God and the ultimate power of love.

As I bring this chapter to a close, I want to make you aware that we are constantly receiving impressions from the planes or realms around us. The physical bodies of each of us emit a most divine aura, as well as the etheric, astral/emotional and mental/psychological. Therefore, we should start each day by invoking the presence of our own higher self, monad, the masters and God. Do take these few seconds daily to align yourself with God and to invoke the presence of protection from all lower auric energies.

Enjoy the awakening of the higher senses and use them always in service of love and for the good of the whole.

7

The Practicality of the Ascension Process

The Ascension Process Is in the Moment

Many advanced lightworkers, evolving at lightning speeds, have forgotten how to enjoy the pure nectar that flows from anchoring in the divine love-and-light quotients. For you, this chapter is a prod to remember.

For the newly awakened disciple or initiate (at least newly awakened this lifetime), the design of this chapter is such that you can rightly view the process of initiation/ascension from the beginning, so that your path is from the outset one of integration and wholeness. In this light you will come to know the process of ascension and the process of descension as one. The higher you go, the more integrated you will become. The more you anchor yourself in heaven, the easier it will be to anchor heaven on Earth and the more joyous the path.

I will not mislead you with the illusion that this path will always be easy, for breaking out of the limitations of one atmosphere into another always has its bumps. This path, however, can always be filled with the incredible lightness of being if you learn from the so-called beginning to commit to the memory of every cell in your body the fact that the ascension process is in the same moment you are.

If you continually keep this attitude of living in the moment, you will be able to fully savor the joys, as well as proceed from that place of integration and synthesis. The concern of getting somewhere along the spiritual path—achieving a particular initiation, anchoring a certain degree of light quotient, reaching the deepest stages of samadhi and so forth—all too often pulls you out of the moment and focuses your attention on a goal that is yet to be achieved. When this becomes the basic attitude, much is lost and the many possible joys, sharings and little things along the way are by-passed altogether.

The question then remains, how do we proceed on our given path? Paramahansa Yogananda said our desire for God needs to be like that of a drowning man who desires air, and yet we must keep ourselves balanced enough to live the moment. There is one simple answer, and that is that the truly integrated path of ascension incorporates at once our utmost desire and attention to the cultivation and activation of the higher energies within us and likewise keeps us living as balanced, functioning God-beings on Earth. The answer therefore is a paradox, yet it is one of the key paradoxes that we are asked to master at this point in our individual and planetary evolution.

I cannot stress this point strongly enough, for it is the dispensation for the new millennium. The balance of moving along our path of initiation and ascension must merge with our daily lives, our development of the four lower bodies and our living in the moment so that an even greater wholeness can be brought forth upon the Earth.

Every age has brought with it new revelations. Looked at from a clear point of view, revelation itself can be seen as a continuing process, as revelation upon revelation continues to unfold in succession, and as varying aspects of the revelation of a particular age continue to unfold. The process of ascension itself is one of the great revelations of this new age period in Earth's unfoldment. Under the umbrella of this great revelation continue to flow numerous insights regarding this process. There are two important revelations along these lines. The first is the understanding that the psychological self must be completely mastered and integrated in service of the Christ consciousness for one to be truly considered a full-fledged ascended master. This is regardless of the level of initiation, light quotient, psychic abilities, channeling abilities, teaching abilities, clairvoyance, leadership or healing abilities. This is one of the least understood yet most important insights lightworkers have yet come to understand. The new term I have coined for this concept is "integrated ascension," not fragmented ascension as my friend Djwhal Khul likes to call it. The second key is that of merging the goal with the moment, thus allowing for the true blending of heaven and earth.

Ultimately, no soul can go past the seventh initiation in its progress unless all the aspects of itself become not only lighted, but integrated with the whole. What the Hierarchy is busy doing now is using every means available to awaken each individual to the parts of him/herself that have been ignored in the hurry to accomplish the goal. I keep being reminded by them to tell all my readers that the path *is* the goal, that all must be viewed as one divine whole and that all psychological aspects must be brought into cohesion within that whole. Therefore, those who are just now beginning to activate certain parts of themselves in order to proceed along the path of light and love will do it in such a manner as to take the *whole* self upon this journey divine. This will allow a whole and integrated journey from the start, keeping initiates centered in the holy moment and allowing for a fuller and more balanced appreciation of the initiatory process. The fragmentation occurring in recent times has resulted from the rapid growth of the spiritual body, while the mental, emotional and physical bodies have not been manifesting an equal level of godliness. The passing of initiations has more to do with the spiritual body than the other three bodies, which is why this misunderstanding of the process has taken place.

To those of us who went charging ahead, we must find joy in the fact that we have been wayshowers into the light. For the vast majority of us (if not all) however, the fact remains that we must go back and integrate the fragmented parts of ourselves that were left unattended as we hurriedly made our way into the seventh sphere and beyond. We had and have an incredibly wonderful puzzle piece, but what is true for those who follow after us is likewise true for us, and what was left unintegrated, unclear, unattended to must be put right.

Please, beloved readers, if you find yourself among this group, do not feel threatened or even inconvenienced in the slightest, for all are able to do this while anchored in the light, love, power and heart of God. We must do this, however, for as parts of the whole it is everyone's responsibility to return to the whole as completely as possible. I guarantee you that all will feel better once this is achieved, for as you align, integrate and merge with the moment and the need of the hour, so too will you feel a unique, new and wonderful sense of completion, synthesis and unity with all that is.

An example of imbalance might be a seventh-degree initiate who has a high degree of light quotient, is a clairaudient channel for the masters and/or spiritual teacher or healer, but on a psychological level has failed the test of power, fame, money and pride. He/she might not be able to work with people because of an eccentric personality, or maybe because he/she is filled with too much negative-ego ambition and anger. This example is not as unusual as one might think. For this reason lightworkers should not get overly confident or inflated over passing higher initiations and even their ascension.

Such little (or great, as the case might be) imbalances that threw us off kilter will be finally and ultimately brought under our mastery. The bumps in the road that kept throwing us off balance will be smoothed over, and we will finally be able to glide through each and every area of our lives. Of course, some areas will be more harmonious with some souls than others, but that is how it should be. The essential point is that none of the areas will be left unattended and fragmented from ourselves.

Likewise, we will realize again that stopping and smelling the roses, as the cliché goes, plays as much a part in our lives as does stargazing. Each moment, if allowed to be lived to the fullest in an integrated and spiritualized sense, will manifest undreamed-of possibilities. The era of the new age will anchor on all the planes of Earth—the physical, etheric, astral/emotional/feeling and the thought/mental realms.

It is true to say that in God there is no time and it is equally true to say that God lives within each and every moment. It is most correct to say that God exists within timelessness yet manifests through and within each and every moment. This realization is what we are now being called to embrace. In the ultimate synthesis of the timeless aspect of God with the living moment of God and the moment-by-moment purification of all bodies within God, we will come to know a completeness—that is the revelation and dispensation for the new millennium.

Relating to People through Spiritual Consciousness

When one follows the path of ascension in this complete way, there is an inevitable total restructuring of how he/she views the world and the ascension process. The way one views the world has a direct effect on how he relates to the world at large and to specific individuals, which combine to create his world.

Since we see the world through either the eyes of the lower self and negative ego or from the perspective of the higher self and monad, we will therefore relate and interrelate with others through either the principle of separateness or of unity. The difference between these two ways of perceiving and interacting is literally the difference between heavenly and hellish states of consciousness.

The practical application of following the conscious and integrated path of ascension becomes clear when considering the following point. If the entire planet's population operated from a place of unity and oneness and interacted with each other individually across the great divide of world religions, races, nationalities and so forth, we would be living in a world that was truly the manifestation of the kingdom of God upon Earth.

We are, however, each of us worlds unto ourselves, and therefore it is up to us individually to *choose* to make the process of ascension real in our lives and in our worlds. I am assuming that those who are reading this book have chosen to make this a reality for themselves. I point out here how practical a reality the ascension process really is. It is all too easy to get lost among the stars and suns of the inner world and to segregate daily living from the initiation/ascension process. But in truth they are one.

When we allow ourselves to bring that down, as it were, and fully incorporate it into our daily living and interacting with others, certain situations that have been either unpleasant or tedious can be truly turned around.

For example, suppose that waiting in a long line at the post office is not your idea of fun. You do, however, have choice about how you handle this situation, which in turn affects the others in line. Tension usually begins to build with subtle sighs, mumblings, grumblings and maybe a few explicatives as huge packages are brought to the counter . . . while the line waits. These are reactions of personalities operating from a separative, negative-ego place within themselves. If you, however, choose to use that time to center in your own higher nature, to call to the masters, to remember that God is all and all pervasive, then your energy field not only protects you from the grumbling nature of those about you, but radiates outward and touches them with the elevated energy of love and patience. At the very least you will remain centered within your own God-self. At the most, your love energy will quiet the storms about you and transform the very atmosphere itself. When you reach the window you will greet the postal worker with a smile, which, I assure you, he/she will most graciously appreciate. And you will have succeeded in turning an entire situation around.

This, of course, applies to any situation of a similar nature. The grocery store does not have to reflect the marketplaces of the Middle Ages. I have been to a few, particularly in some of the boroughs of New York, that were veritable throwbacks to medieval times. Lightworkers, do not confine your divine connection to your meditation periods alone. Bring it out and about with you to the marketplace, where your sense of unity, peace, love and oneness are truly needed.

In the Corporate World

The corporate world has been structured to be a world unto itself. Unfortunately this world has been mostly operating out of greed, egotism, self-centeredness, callousness, competition and even downright cruelty. This is a world where money is God, and there shall be no other God before it. Like any other world, however, it is simply the reflection of the state of consciousness of the people who dwell within it and those who run it. But it too is subject to change by the integration of those operating from God-consciousness.

There are those of you whose puzzle piece puts you right in the heart of corporate structure, and it is up to you who are working your path of ascension while functioning within this particular sphere to effectuate the needed changes. This is your divine mission.

I am not saying to storm to the head of your particular structure and demand a new policy reflective of the light-and-love levels and personal transformation you are going through. Please do not misunderstand me on this matter, because I am not suggesting this. What I am suggesting is that you operate from the highest place possible, right where you currently are. I don't care if you are the head of some great conglomerate or if you are making copies at a copy machine, the essential point I am getting at is that you begin right where you are at to demonstrate what you have received in your ascension process—allow it to come through as you interact with your co-workers and go about your day. Office work has the tendency to get us harried because there often are deadlines and pressure that cannot possibly be accommodated by man, woman or machine. Your job, as a person on the path of practical ascension, is to do the best you can without buying into the corporate mindset, and to demonstrate God as best your given situation allows without alienating those who are stuck in the third-dimensional materialistic mind.

Clearly, a suit-and-tie office is not the proper place to begin a discourse on the science of meditation, initiation and ascension. Yet I am hard pressed to find a better place to teach these principles by demonstrating them through a smile, politeness and holding an attitude of inner calmness and kindness. What and who we are speaks much more loudly than what we say we are. If each of us can simply be that higher self to the best of our ability in this type of situation, then we are truly on the way to changing the world. It is much more important to be and demonstrate God than it is just to talk about it, specifically in a situation when words would fall on deaf ears.

An image of the ripples from a single pebble thrown into a lake comes to mind. Yes, we might be but a single pebble, but centered in our divine natures we are as a diamond pebble, each with the ability to generate enough small ripples by letting our diamond natures shine forth to eventually change the world. We also have the benefit of knowing that while we are doing this, we are ourselves moving ever closer to the center of our own beingness in God.

Ascension and Relationships

There is truly no greater accelerator on the path of ascension than a romantic relationship. This is likewise one of the greatest and most direct areas in which to experience the practicality of the ascension/initiation process. When we are dealing with our partner and/or mates we tend to take for granted or become just a bit too comfortable, conveniently forgetting all that we previously acquired during our growth processes. My strong suggestion is that you use this particular type of relationship to manifest your divine potential to the highest possible degree.

When you are dealing with your romantic partner, all the little stuff of life tends to surface. Each moment offers ample opportunity to choose from which level of your being you will function. Will you act or react? Will you take the time to connect with your highest spiritual self before attempting communication, or will you just let it all hang out, so to speak? Will you even remember to communicate at all, or will you fall into the trap that the majority of couples do—assume your mate to be a mindreader? From these few examples you can see that this area comes complete with abundant opportunities to act either from your God-self or from the lower self and negative ego.

One essential area where ascension can be aided through the romantic relationship is communication. People in relationships often forget to communicate, or when they do it is from the personality level and lower self. I recommend that the lines of communication be kept open at all times, but that partners never attempt communication during the heat of emotion. Only after they cool down should the two sit together and simultaneously call upon their higher selves. This can be done while holding hands. Once that divine hookup is established, then they should begin to discuss things from the calm, clear center of their spiritual selves. You would be amazed at what can be accomplished through this simple technique.

Once you can communicate properly, feelings do not need to be pushed down and tucked away until they reach an emotional boiling point. Every area of the relationship—from who does the laundry, handling finances to sexual intimacy—can be discussed calmly and rationally and from the God-self within. No area needs to be judged by the lower consciousness as either too little or too big, but rather the relationship is seen to be one functioning whole that encompasses every aspect of itself within a sphere of open and spiritualized communication.

Ascension and the Family Unit

Expanding from the concept of romantic relationship into that of the family unit itself is really a simple matter. As children are brought into the picture, you simply include them in the practical daily practicing of your process of initiation and ascension. Having children is, by its very nature, an initiation in itself. The relationship between parent and child is complex and touches parts of each that nothing in the world seems able to access.

The choice, however, is the same as that within the romantic relationship from which the child was first brought into the world. Do you react from your negative ego and lower self, or do you act from your higher self/monadic level of spiritual beingness? Our children are truly souls who have come through us due to the operation of karmic law and karmic ties.

They offer us great opportunity for growth and the expression of God in its highest form. They likewise offer us great opportunities in which to *lose it*. Children, from the higher self's perspective, are the ultimate spiritual test of one's achievement of Christ consciousness. Romantic relationships would be a close second. If you can remain unconditionally loving, firm, patient, forgiving, nonjudgmental and retain appropriate boundaries within these relationships, then you have truly achieved self-realization on the psychological level.

The nuclear family is itself a microcosm of the greater macrocosm of the family of God to which all of humanity belongs. Within this microcosm we can use each opportunity to connect with the higher self/monad before we act or react. Likewise we can use all these tools to master our four lower bodies so that we relate to our children and nuclear family as a whole from the clearest, most purified, highly attuned physical/etheric, astral/feeling and mental/ thought bodies.

If we have chosen to be part of a romantic relationship and continue to expand into a full household with children, pets and all that that world brings with it, we have indeed expanded our world into a fully functioning microcosm of the larger family of humankind. How well that microcosm functions is up to all of its participating parts. While at first it is the parents who set the tone, creating the healthiest, most spiritualized environment of which they are capable, eventually the children (who are actually adult souls who have come back into the world as infants and babies) will themselves come into their own. All of the family then will have specific parts to play in how the family unit functions as a whole.

Whether you are child or parent, or are living in a household where you are at once child and parent, you are ultimately soul/monad. How you relate and interact with each other is how God is interrelating within the microcosm of which you are a part. Therefore it is suggested that you use this little world within the world to make your process of ascension a grounded reality and to function as the godlike being that you truly are.

Ascension in the World of the Artist

The variegated medium of the arts offers great opportunity to integrate, express and bring the process of ascension into practice and manifestation. Both "art" and "ascension" seem to carry within their very essence the nature of that which is impractical, but this could not be further from the truth.

The power of the arts cannot be disputed. Through the ages forms of art have brought many an otherwise stoic man to tears. The power of religious painting and sculpture have uplifted humanity by the very viewing of it—high enough, if only for a moment, to contact and connect with the of spirit. Often the paintings, stained glass windows or sculptures of a cathedral have done more to bring people to their knees and lift their souls to the heavens than the most beautiful sermon. Pinnacles can be seen in Michelangelo's Sistine Chapel ceiling, statue of David and the Pietà.

Yet words themselves, when divinely inspired, have had and still have a profound effect. I have been told by several people that their first experience of God was in reading the poetry of Khalil Gibran, Kabir, William Blake or William Wordsworth. This does not even include the power of the word as written in the New Testament or other spiritual scriptures of a variety of cultures.

Music and words combine to form the sounds celestial under the creative power of the world's great composers. The masses of Johann Sabastian Bach, the *Requiem* of Mozart, Handel's *Messiah* and Beethoven's ninth symphony have functioned as direct elevators to God since they were first brought into creation. These are just some of the better-known spiritually uplifting combinations of music and voice. We can span the gamut from opera to popular song and see the power contained within this medium. This is equally true when considering the more commercial forms of art. Daily television programs as well as more intricately composed films touch almost all civilized life to one degree or another. The world of the arts can be a very powerful tool of practical expression of ascension or it can function as a slide that cascades its audience into the realms of the negative ego.

The Artist As Cocreator with God

One important thing to note when discussing the effect that art has upon us is just who the artist is, what that artist or group of artists is trying to say and where the work is designed to take us. Consider for example films like *E.T.* and *King of Kings* and compare them with *Hellraiser* and *Nightmare on Elm Street*. One type of film is clearly designed to lift the spirits of the viewer, while the other is designed to tap into the negative ego and feed it with horrible imagery. It is clear that one must use discrimination when deciding on which movie to see.

There are, of course, movies that fall in the middle, simply seeking to entertain, while others explore human nature or look at history. Certain films—not of the exploitational variety—contain violence and/or dark and disturbing imagery, and yet their cumulative effect uplifts the human spirit. Good examples are *The Elephant Man*, *The Hunchback of Notre Dame* with Charles Laughton and *Schindler's List*. All contain dark, disturbing elements yet are ultimately moving, elevating experiences. The tragedies of Shakespeare are also perfect examples. I am not trying to tell you which films to see or not to see, but by the nature of their titles and one-minute trailers you can tell certain films are made only to tap into the lowest regions, putting forth fear and terror and leaving little to the imagination. These types of films I definitely advise against for those on the path of initiation and ascension.

The power that the artist has is enormous indeed. While we are all cocreators with God, artists can be more easily seen to act as cocreator with God than others. Seeing life from various viewpoints, artists should be free to express and communicate their vision with us, but as souls on the path of initiation and ascension we also have the responsibility to choose what to take in from the vast array available.

The world of the artist offers many opportunities for the practical application of the path of ascension. While too often the world of art is viewed as an impractical world of the imagination, it is quite practical indeed, serving as an important tool in the unfolding of God's plan on Earth.

Ascension and the Political Arena

The people who hold the highest offices of nations form the basic structure within which the world functions. Very often, however, a spiritually focused individual will find no place to even consider the political arena, much less participate within it. Thankfully, with the coming in of the seventh ray, this is all going to change. This is something that must change, because as I have so vehemently brought to your attention, the process of ascension is a process of integrating the whole as much as it is a process of reaching ever-expanded heights of spiritual beingness.

The fragmentation that exists between these two aspects of what in truth are aspects of the same whole is seen most acutely when looking at the world of politics. Many lightworkers would prefer to leave that specific arena to "them" and focus exclusively on the more meditative and glamorous aspects of initiation. This path might have seemed to work in the past, but as the clarion call now is to integrate ascension with descension—to merge the process of initiation with that of integrating the parts within the greater whole—this fragmented perspective on spiritual life no longer works.

We are now at a point in the history of humanity's development where they who seek to embrace the one must be willing to embrace the many aspects that comprise the one. The political world and the world of nations and governments is part and parcel of our world, and they must be viewed thusly.

Obviously, it is not everyone's calling to participate actively in the world of governments by virtue of seeking office. It is time, however, for all of us to become involved in the political arena. No matter what nation we live in, we should play an active role in bringing the most highly evolved beings into office. This requires being aware, at least aware enough to make some decision about whom you feel is most aligned with Hierarchical intent. I would never venture to tell anyone how to vote, but I will say (no matter what the policy of your nation might be), pay attention.

When voting, or playing whatever part is appropriate in your particular government, I advise looking for qualities that are indicative of souls who have moved far enough along their paths of initiation/ascension to hold to the principles of the higher self. Some qualities indicative of this type of leader are:

1. True compassion
2. Integrity
3. An honest desire to serve
4. An ability to hold a position of leadership, while at the same time being one of the people
5. A belief in God
6. Inner strength
7. A good heart
8. The ability to love
9. Decisiveness
10. Clarity
11. Trustworthiness
12. Open mindedness
13. Humanitarian attitude
14. Nonattacking attitude toward political opponents
15. Ability to transcend partisan politics

Base your decision upon these divine qualities, rather than on allegiance to this or that party. Listen to those running for office with the intuition of your soul/monad and you will be guided to act accordingly.

Summary

The ascension process is one of the most practical things an individual can be involved with. Despite its seeming preoccupation with the spiritual realm, when seen rightly it is not a preoccupation with the realm of spirit apart from the realm of form, but a true and practical integration of the world of spirit within the world of form.

The path of initiation and ascension is also a path of descension. It is bringing spirit into form and form into spirit. It is the upraising of the four lower bodies and the calling forth of the highest frequencies into those four bodies. Initiation might be rightly called integration and synthesis, for, as I have said, the two are but halves of the same whole. As each of our bodies rises ever higher into the light, so the light is then anchored into and infused within our physical bodies and the very Earth herself.

The belief system that holds to the thought that the spiritual is separate from the physical must give way to the clear seeing that what we have in the past called spiritual is in fact spirit essence at one with and within all worlds, only functioning at higher and higher, lighter and ever-more inclusive vibrations or frequencies. The phrase "God is all and that I Am" is true at every level of being. Therefore, the higher we go, the more we embrace the fullness of the Earth and the All. In the process we become practical expressions of spirit upon the realm of form. Even as we learn to rise up and embrace our bodies of light, so we learn to integrate that light and love within the world in which we live, move and have our being—and that world is the one world of God. This is the divine plan of God—to create heaven on Earth—a new world of integratively ascended beings fully participating in all aspects of Earth life.

8

Thought and the Power of the Spoken Word

Throughout all religious traditions runs the common theme: watch what you say. There have been many interpretations of the opening statement in the gospel of John in the Bible, "In the beginning was the Word and the Word was with God and the Word was God." As is often the case, these statements have many meanings simultaneously. Let us for our particular discussion explore this quote in as direct a perspective as possible, seeing "the word" to mean quite literally the spoken word of God and humanity as the sons and daughters of God.

The ultimate unity between humanity and God is a fact. Since this is so, humanity is indeed the microcosm of the greater macrocosm of All That Is, or God. With that in mind, let us incorporate another biblical statement of great impact from Genesis: "And God said, let there be light, and there was light." Thus it is by the power of the word, which is an aspect of God, that all comes forth into manifestation.

With such awesome power within us, it is amazing to listen to the trite and casual way in which our words are thrown about. We use words all the time, but often even the most advanced initiate will not pause to take the effect of those words into consideration. Letting the negative ego take control or operate on automatic pilot, words often flow from the tongue with little or no thought, sending forces of negativity that one moment's consideration could certainly prevent.

Healing Words versus Harmful Words

One of my favorite Sai Baba sayings is that the mind creates bondage or the mind creates liberation. This is equally true in regard to the spoken word—words can harm or words can heal. They do just that. Often words are simply wasted in idle speech, causing an unnecessary expenditure of energy that could be put to far better use bringing a specific objectified creation or plan into manifestation or action. It is not, however, the casual word I wish to discuss but rather the word that creates untold destruction in its wake.

Words of negativity are not the vague and nebulous things many believe them to be. While it remains ultimately true that all ascended masters and advanced initiates (or indeed anyone on guard) can protect themselves from the force of the negative word, it does require effort and a constantly vigilant guard against this onslaught. While I would most definitely recommend this to everyone it is especially important that those upon the conscious path of ascension/initiation guard their tongues and watch what they say.

Gossip

Gossip is one of the cruelest ways words can be used against another person. These words carry with them an often untrue thought form, which is not only sent directly toward the targeted individual, but grows like a snowball rolling downhill as it is passed from person to person. It begins as a thought based on a judgment one person makes about another and then let loose via lips and tongue like so many poison darts. The basic fact is that more often than not, words of gossip are not related to truth but only to the faulty perception of an individual's negative ego. These faulty poisoned darts then pass from person to person, accumulating more and more poison as these words continue to make their rounds. By the time they hit the ear of the target person, they are so poisonous and have done so much needless damage that they hit their mark with the force of a cannon.

Unless the targeted individual is standing in the full armor of psychic defense with no human weaknesses, this gossip is bound to affect him/her in one way or another. Beloved readers, although I encourage the practice of protective psychic defense and holding the mind ever steady in the light, I likewise support the reality that we should all be free to live in a state of receptive spirituality. None of us should have to live in a state of constant guard against gossip because none of us should be indulging in such negative practices.

Words, as I said before, contain great power. To consciously abuse words, particularly if you are on the path of initiation, is a definite misuse of power. Although the bulk of humanity looks on gossip as a harmless practice, it is not harmless and indeed most destructive. Whether or not the person being gossiped about learns of this consciously (and they almost always do), these negative thought forms do find their way into the person's aura, causing a certain degree of discomfort until they are psychically removed. If they do make their way into the individual's conscious awareness, this person must not only deal with the destruction upon a psychic level, but also on a psychological level. This can be painful and time consuming and is certainly unnecessary.

If you find that you have an issue with another person, realize that it lies within your better judgment to simply address the issue with that person and discuss it from a calm, rational and spiritually attuned space or just don't say anything. Don't relegate it to the world of gossip, where it will inevitably turn into a force of destruction. Stop and put yourself in the other person's shoes. Would you rather have a heart-to-heart talk with your friend or would you rather be the target of vicious gossip? I'm sure you would prefer that your friend came to you directly rather than began speaking about you behind your back. Think before you speak, and take special care not to initiate speech in the harmful form of gossip.

Other Negative Talk

Those of us who go about the day speaking negatively about either ourselves or others are creating very definite atmospheric disturbances. Just as words take shape in etheric matter, as do thoughts; in one regard there is little difference between them. Words, however, are also heard, and if they are of a negative nature do much to create more of the already-prevalent noise pollution. Noise pollution is not just the loud sounds of city life, but also the negative repetition of words, ideas, judgments and condemnations that fill our mental atmosphere daily. Trust me, this is more damaging than a loud truck or blasting boom box.

One way this type of negativity manifests is through the constant grumbling and complaining about a given day's events. Too much time is spent verbalizing, reliving and reactivating what one perceives to be the wrong actions of another or of a given situation. Thus you often have members of a couple, who finally arrive home after a long day at work, going over and over every negative aspect and experience they felt subjected to during that day.

The interesting thing about this situation is that the couple could have chosen to perceive the day's events as lessons to learn from rather than negative experiences others put them through. If this were done, the conversation could be geared toward what could be gained from these experiences, rather than toward simple complaining. I am not necessarily saying that certain situations are not unpleasant, nor am I saying that others in a work or social environment should be granted impunity for expressing negative behavior toward you, or that couples or friends should not have the freedom to get these experiences off their chests. What I am saying, is that once expressed, constant complaining and grumbling continues to feed the negative experience, so that it grows rather than heals.

When indulging in constant complaining, rehashing negative experiences, judging others or cussing at the world, you build up a polluted mental and psychic atmosphere in your home and in your aura. This adds to whatever the problem might be, creating more of the very thing you objected to in the first place. If allowed to continue, this ultimately infuses your own aura with so much negativity that it creates a psychic life of its own, lingering long after the original problem has been satisfactorily dealt with and obliterated. Therefore, dear readers, I caution you against this behavior lest you create for yourself that which you dislike in others. Ultimately, you will be left with the task of clearing out from within your own psychic field the debris you were seeking to heal and relieve in the first place.

Being Vigilant

Watching one's speech does require a certain degree of vigilance. One area where the most vigilance is required is at home among family and friends, when we are most relaxed.

Couples and family members often fall into almost unconscious patterns of put-downs and under-the-breath negative comments. Unfortunately, when this occurs the subconscious mind begins to believe them. This is particularly the case where small children, who have not yet developed the means to put up psychic self-defense systems, are involved, but is extremely damaging for anyone.

Among our family and friends, and especially when we are alone with our mate, we do not want to be on guard the entire time. There is enough self-protecting we must do out in the world without continuing that mode at home. So monitoring our speech patterns so that they hold no strong or destructive elements pays off in positive speech that ultimately becomes automatic as breathing.

Negative Thinking

Negative thinking works in much the same way as the above examples of negative speaking. The main difference is that while the spoken word takes shape in the physical/auditory realm, the thought remains in the etheric/astral/mental realm. Both word and thought infiltrate the auras of both the speaker/thinker and the one to whom that thought or word is directed. They both, through the law of attraction, call what is dwelt upon into manifestation—a most important point to consider.

The great philosopher and teacher Hermes said that all is mind; the universe is mental. It therefore follows that the thoughts we create in turn create what for us constitutes our universe. So before indulging in any sort of negative thinking, we should remind ourselves that we are cocreators with God, and that one of our most potent means of creating is via the mind. If we do this, then we shall find it much easier to choose not to indulge in constantly manipulating negative thought patterns, but rather turn our attention to what is most positive in our lives. The affirmations in this book are wonderful tools to repattern negative thoughts.

Just as we build our physical homes, picking out pieces of furniture and arranging them in pleasing patterns, so too we build our mental homes by the thoughts we think on a moment-to-moment basis. Out of these thought patterns we likewise construct our auras, our physical bodies and even the circumstances we draw into our lives. The fact is we have the ability to build palaces as well as prisons if we simply keep guard over what we say and thus reprogram our mental thoughts/worlds.

Healing Thoughts, Words and Sounds

There are spiritual tools such as chants or mantras that can help us attune to our higher selves, monads and our pure state of spiritual being. Throughout the ages in a wide variety of religious and spiritual practices, mantras or chants have been used in order to receive the desired effect. The most familiar mantra of the East is the chanting of the sound *om* or *aum.*

Entering into a meditative state and turning within, the student of yoga is guided to either verbally or silently intone the *om* or *aum* sound. This has a soothing effect, eventually leading to a place of mental and emotional quietude. Likewise it helps attune the meditator to the sound of life itself, or God. Much power is in this particular mantra, which both invigorates and calms. I highly recommend you give it a try. When you wish to give the mind a rest from itself, try the following meditation.

Om Meditation

Find a comfortable posture, either lying down or sitting up, keeping the spine erect. Follow the natural flow of the breath for a moment or two as you settle into the stillness.

Take a deep breath, filling first the lower abdomen, then the upper abdomen and finally the chest. As you breathe out, let the breath carry first the ooooooo sound for two-thirds of the outbreath and then follow with the mmmmmmm sound. Therefore, as the air is expelled from first the chest and then the upper abdomen, you will chant oooooooooo. As the air is expelled from the lower abdomen, chant the mmmmmmm sound.

Pause, if you need to, to allow a natural breath to flow. After a while this will not be necessary, but never force anything. So at first make sure to take the time you need between chanting the om.

Then begin the process of the three-part inbreath and the chanting of om on the three-part outbreath once again.

Try your best to be as rhythmically consistent as possible, so that neither the chant nor the breath is fragmented or broken.

In the beginning of your practice, do this a maximum of three times aloud before spending a couple of minutes repeating the sound silently while the breath flows naturally. You may slowly build up the amount of time you actually chant the om aloud, but remember not to force it and by no means exceed ten minutes unless you have been guided by an instructor or have taken classes in breath control and yoga.

You can feel free to sit up to 45 minutes listening to the om inwardly, as the breath flows naturally. Allow the breath to be quite natural, and remember to fully ground yourself on Earth before you bring this (or any) meditation to a close. Then stretch your limbs, open your eyes, give yourself a moment to adjust and go about the day with a calm, quiet, spiritually attuned mind.

The Prayer of St. Francis

One of the most beautiful prayers is the prayer of Saint Francis. This is both a prayer and an affirmation that, repeated aloud and/or silently, is one of the best tools of attitudinal healing combined with prayer I know. I give to you here the meat of this prayer, so that it can be easily used as a meditation/affirmation.

Lord make me an instrument of Thy peace;

Where there is hatred, let me sow love;

Where there is injury, pardon;

Where there is doubt, faith;

Where there is darkness, light;

Where there is sadness, joy.

(It's interesting to note that Saint Francis of Assisi was a former incarnation of master Kuthumi.)

Elohim/Yod He Vau He

The elohim are the beings God created to help Him build the infinite universe. The Kabbalah refers to the elohim as the divine Mother, and also as being one of the most powerful of all names. The Kabbalah also refers to Yod He Vau He as the divine Father. Combining the chanting of both these powernames or sounds makes an amazing mantra, which at once embraces the feminine and masculine aspects of creation.

When chanting these names assume a comfortable position with the back straight. The straight-back posture is important because the energy moves upward along the spine; slumping or slouching impedes the energy flow. Once you are comfortable, simply begin by following the breath a bit, then slowly chant the name "elohim" in a long drawn-out fashion. It would sound something like *elll-oooo-heeem*. Follow this by slowly chanting "yod-he-vau-he," which sounds like *yohd-hay-voh-hay*. Then repeat this for as long as it feels comfortable. When you feel like quieting down, give yourself a minute or two to chant these names inwardly. Allow yourself a few moments then to experience the quiet, tranquil recesses to which these most potent words have brought you. As always, ground yourself fully to the Earth before you come out of meditation.

Holy Prayers of Various Religions

The power of holy prayers of any world religion to which you feel most attuned can work wonders in transforming your mental system and indeed your entire four-body system. By saying such prayers or chanting mantras you are using *the word* as a cocreator with God, intoning the highest-possible vibrational frequencies. Other wonderful examples of healing words are the Hail Mary, the Lord's Prayer, *om* shanti shanti shanti (*shanti* means "peace" in Hinduism), chanting the name of Buddha, Christ or any of the great masters, repeating "I Am that I Am" or chanting "Sai Baba/Sai Ram." One of the most powerful and beautiful prayers is the Great Invocation by master Djwhal Khul through Alice A. Bailey in *Ponder on This*.

"From the point of light within the mind of God
Let light stream forth into the minds of men.
Let light descend on Earth.

"From the point of love within the heart of God
Let love stream forth into the hearts of men.
May Christ return to Earth.

"From the center where the will of God is known
Let purpose guide the little wills of men,
The purpose which the masters know and serve.

"From the center which we call the race of men
Let the plan of love and light work out
And may it seal the doors where evil dwells.

"Let light and love and power
Restore the plan on Earth."

All of the above serve as healing balms, not only to you, but to the world itself as these sounds, words, mantras and prayers move through you out into the etheric, astral and mental atmosphere. The choice lies with us, my beloved readers, whether we are going to use words and thoughts to hurt or to heal. It is my fervent prayer that each of us chooses to use the power of thought, word and deed in order to effectuate as rapid a healing as possible within ourselves and upon the planet.

9

The Devic Line of Evolution
The Reality of Angels

So far in this book much has been discussed about the esoteric nature of humanity as we evolve into the higher aspects of our God-selves. What I have not discussed until now is the role that the angelic, or devic, line of evolution plays in relationship to our own. As much of the teaching conveyed to you in these pages involves the process of synthesis and integration, so must the devic or angelic line of evolution be synthesized as part of the whole picture, for the part it plays is great indeed!

The devas, as they are called throughout much occult literature, are the builders of form within the universe. The devic line of evolution is one that runs parallel with that of humanity; it likewise runs the gamut of various stages of development along that pathway. There are graded ranks of devas, from those who work almost blindly, functioning as it were within the aura of one of the more developed devas, to those great and powerful devas, or archangels, whose cosmic job involves helping build the outer expression or form of the very cosmos itself.

As we can say a person is at this or that level of initiation, so the evolving angel can be compared to a first-, second- or seventh-degree initiate. Likewise, as there are less-evolved members of humanity, so you have what in occult literature are called wood sprites, fairies and gnomes. And just as there are those who evolved through the seven levels of initiation, so too are there the great building devas or angels, who are the divine architects of worlds. The main point is that at every level, the two lines of evolution overlap, each contributing their specific part to the whole.

In folklore, angels and devas have long been known as reality. Throughout the ages little elfish beings have been reported to have been seen in the Highlands of Scotland, in the English countryside and amidst the lush woodlands. They have also populated our children's storybooks, and images of winged angels have soothed many children to sleep. However, until fairly recently, angels were not taken very seriously, with certain of the great archangels of the Bible the only exception to that general rule.

Now, as I sit and type this, I notice the pictures of angels that I have adorning my room. Less than twenty years ago this would not have been the case. Now angel bookmarks, cards, clocks, watches, posters, statues and even T-shirts are available in stores. People are beginning, en masse, to sense the reality of the angelic kingdom.

Angels and devas are indeed real. They are becoming a recognized reality because humanity is meant to work in much closer cooperation with them than we have in the past. The devic rate of vibrational frequency is more etherialized than that of current humanity, which is one reason that they are not readily seen by us. This is changing, however, as our own frequencies change and all of us learn to see into the etheric realms more clearly.

This is the third time in history that this has occurred. The first was during the biblical era; the second, during the medieval era; and the third, this present era. It is vital to keep in mind that we stand at the threshold of a new millennium, bringing with it a thrust of new energies. Likewise, it introduces a new revelation of energy patterns that were accessed at other crucial times throughout history. This, however, will occur at a higher turn of the spiral, as all moves onward and upward.

A practical reason that we have not been able to see the devic kingdom to the degree we could in the past is that as humanity became industrialized, civilized to the point of destroying much of nature's natural abundance, the devic and angelic beings withdrew into areas of densely forested seclusion. The atmosphere that humanity has created is poisonous to the devas and destructive to their work. This is particularly so when considering those who work with the plant kingdom. And so, understandably enough, they have moved to safer ground.

Slowly, and almost against our will, humanity is waking up to the fact that the world it created is not only poisonous to the devic creatures but to ourselves as well. As more of us begin to change the way we relate to Mother Earth, begin to demonstrate that which our initiatory process has revealed as higher truth, take environmental action and take all kingdoms and evolutions into our awareness, so will we slowly turn things around and fulfill our divine destiny. And this includes working in conscious cooperation with the devic/angelic kingdom.

Overview of the Angelic Hierarchy

The *elementals,* as they are called in occult literature, are the spiritual essences out of which all forms are built. They are composed out of the mind-stuff of a higher angel. In actuality, the elemental kingdom itself evolves in graded ranks, and there are those better known as fairies, gnomes, wood sprites, salamanders and sylphs who are much further along their evolutionary structure and will one day individualize. This is also true of certain animals, who will at the appropriate hour become the humanity of a future age. (This subject gets quite specific and will be dealt with later in this book). Suffice it to say for now, the experience of many elemental entities is like that of many beings in the animal kingdom, insofar as their individual experiences are added into a group soul, and en masse they contribute to the evolution of that entire soul-body before their own individualization process has begun. Their process of individualization is quite different from ours but is specific nonetheless. Remember, they are of an evolution parallel to our own.

As the elemental life is controlled by either a higher grade of angel or overlighting angel (e.g., an angel responsible for the growth of all types of squash), so too is the elemental kingdom responsive to the thoughts of humanity. Humanity creates thought forms and emotional forms depending on what it collectively thinks and feels. That is why it is said that thoughts are things and strong negative emotions do indeed wound. When strong emotion accompanies a thought or feeling, that specific thought/feeling draws around it the elemental essences, which, in turn, give it shape and form within the etheric realm. Once these thoughts take form, they assume a so-called life of their own. Thoughts of anger and hatred shoot like darts at lightning speed, and, if unprotected, the person at whom they are directed take them into his/her etheric body.

Tools for Protection from Negative Thought Forms

1. Call upon Archangel Michael with his blue-flame sword of protection and his legion of angels. He will guard you against negative elemental thought forms with his shield of divine protection. Michael is one of the great protectors and providers of strength for all humanity. It is a good idea to call forth his assistance each day, especially when confronted with any form of negativity. This protection is equally helpful in difficult world situations. Any time the nation or city where you live is going through an undue period of unrest and upheaval, do call upon him for his assistance.

2. Calling upon Christ is likewise one of the most wonderful tools of protection available to humanity. The vibration of Christ/Jesus, Lord Maitreya/Sananda is of such a high order that it will guard you against any negative onslaughts. You can also call upon Mother Mary in the same way. The pure white light of the Virgin Mary and the Christ is an impenetrable armor of protection.

3. You should likewise feel free to call upon God or any master with whom you feel connected. They are there in loving service, awaiting your call.

4. Call upon the very heart of love itself, and wear that heart as you would an outer garment, to surround and protect you as you go about the day. In truth, there is no greater protection than that of love itself. Love is the greatest barrier between you and negative influences, both from outer sources and from the subconscious mind within you. Love is likewise the great purifier; it can cleanse, heal and soothe. "Perfect love casts out all fear"—and all negativity as well. Therefore, throw all negative energy into the rose/white flame of love, and a divine healing and state of protection cannot help but manifest on all levels of your being.

5. This last tool I advise you to use, or to "reactivate," about three times a day. Surround yourself with the golden/white semipermeable bubble of protection that I spoke of earlier. Because this bubble is semipermeable, it allows some of the more loving thoughts and energies that are sent your way to come easily into your auric field and uplift you.

Eliminating Negative Thought Forms

Despite our best efforts, just through the process of living upon this planet, all of us at some point have picked up some negative thought forms and elemental energies that we would do well to be without. There are ways to clear them from your aura that I have expanded on in other books. Here are a few short-cut methods to cleanse your auric field:

1. Ask to be taken to Djwhal Khul's synthesis ashram to be cleared of all negative elemental imprints or thought forms.

2. Ask the Lord of Arcturus and Vywamus for their golden dome of protection in order to both protect and clear you of unwanted negative thought forms. Then ask that any remaining negative energy be vacuumed up and out of the golden dome of protection, thus cleansing out your entire auric field.

3. Call upon Saint Germain to clear away any misqualified energies from within your auric field by the power of the violet transmuting flame.

These are but a few of the tools available to work with, but they are sure to get you on your way in the proper cleansing of your auric fields.

Devas, Nature Spirits, Elementals and the Growing of a Flower

Let us indulge our imaginations and see into the devic kingdom enough to behold the growing of a particular flower. Let us imagine it to be a red rose. The idea for the red rose would, first of all, originate within the mind of the angel/deva of that rose. This particular deva would be one of the many creative building devas who fall under the influence of the over-lighting deva of all roses. Nevertheless, we shall proceed to imagine this one particular deva holding to the idea of his creation-to-be—the red rose.

The deva of the red rose, as I shall call this shining one, puts forth into the world of etheric matter a piece of itself from which to build the form. This piece of itself can be described as a packet of energy made of ele-mental essence. The little building devas then go forth to build this rose, for they too comprise this basic elemental energy. The etheric building de-vas have the power to step down the vibration of the flower until it takes physical root and physical form. (Actually, it is first brought forth from the seed, as you well know.) This they can do with the help of the deva of the red rose, whose work proceeds under the influence of the overlighting deva of all roses. It is at that specific point of manifestation that the so-called fairy is drawn to the rose to tend it and nurture it along in beauty. Thus you have the glorious red rose.

The Elohim

Before moving to a more in-depth look at the way angels interact with our line of evolution and aid us in every area of our life, I must include the elohim. Elohim is one of the power names of God in the Bible and in *The Book of Knowledge: Keys of Enoch*. They are referred to as those beings who created the world by the will of God (YHWH). These beings are of a very high order and, together with the angels, form the right and left hands of God. The following is a list of the elohim (the cocreator gods):

1. Hercules and Amazonia
2. Apollo and Lumina
3. Heros and Amora
4. Purity and Astrea
5. Cyclopia and Virginia
6. Peace and Aloha
7. Arturus and Victoria

There is great power in calling upon these beings and even in the re-citing of their names. Since we are focusing on the angels, and many at-tributes of the elohim are yet shrouded in mystery, I will not go into a de-tailed discussion here. They must, however, be mentioned, for they play a great role in bringing forth the manifestation of the cosmos itself, and much energy can be obtained by simply pronouncing their holy names. Although the part they play, in truth, reaches far beyond our small planet and into the vast universe, if you call for their assistance, they will indeed add the presence of their beingness to yours. Please do count them among the blessed beings who await your call.

As the archangels and the elohim have played a part in the very creation of our universe and the cosmos itself (and certainly our world), they naturally play a vital role in the lives of humanity. Although the angelic kingdom works in graded ranks as does the Hierarchy of masters, the angels are, in truth, available to us throughout the many levels of their hierarchy of being.

The Archangels

The archangels are also known as the overlighting angels because they watch over, or overlight, large groups of angels, humanity and specific areas of activity. Archangel Michael who is working closely with humanity at this time, is an angel of great strength. His function and joy is protecting us with his strength. He has appeared to many people holding a blue-flame sword and many artists have been moved to paint him. There are some people with whom he has established a direct line of communication and through whom he speaks to humanity at large.

Lord Michael, as he is also referred to, is available to any of us who choose to invoke his divine presence. Legions of spiritual angel warriors, so to speak, work directly under him to help humankind fight the battle of light. Whenever you are in a situation where you feel that strength and protection against negativity is what you need, call upon the blessed name of Archangel Michael and his legions. He is also one of the great angels who are easily accessible to all who seek them and can readily be contacted in periods of meditation. Michael is as available for guidance as well as for protection, and I strongly suggest that you avail yourself of his wondrous gifts.

Archangel Raphael is the archangel of healing. As indicated in the chart of the archangels, he works in conjunction with beloved Mother Mary. Their presence overlights all institutions and centers for healing, and there are many healing angels who work under their direct guidance and lineage.

If you find yourself in need of healing, please know that you are not alone nor at the tender mercies of medical science alone. No one is ever truly alone, but the trick is to access the divine beings who so very much want to serve. If you are aware that they are here for you, then they can work with you in greater and deeper ways, simply for the asking.

When someone you love falls ill, know that you can call upon these divine beings for aid and comfort. Commune with them from the depth of your heart. Call upon them and their power to heal will increase ten thousandfold! This is because they, as the masters, can do just so much and no more without being directly asked. The divine law states that there is to be no interference with human free will, and all divine beings obey this law.

As general practice I consult my loved one or friend physically when possible, and on the inner planes, when that is more appropriate, to find out if his/her higher self wants assistance from a specific master or angel-worker. The answer is usually a resounding yes, although sometimes it is no. I do this to respect the law of noninfringement upon the free will of another. When the answer is yes, then I proceed to pray and invoke the divine intervention of these two beloved archangels of healing on that person's behalf. I never try to order them to effectuate a cure, but I ask them to use whatever means possible to alleviate suffering and to help the healing process. It is the joy of beloved Archangel Raphael and Mother Mary to do this, and the person almost immediately senses some relief and comfort come into his being.

Remember, when calling upon these wonderful beings, do so with as much heart as possible. The energies that the angelic kingdom as a whole most respond to are that of feeling. Therefore, call them in such a manner and they will not fail to respond.

I have given you a somewhat detailed description involving the invocation of archangels Raphael, Mary and Michael, whose feminine counterpart is Faith. Here is a brief list of all archangels, each of whom is associated with a specific ray and has a special line of work and service. In invoking them please use the same intensity of heart.

RAY	ARCHANGEL	QUALITY OF SERVICE
First ray	Michael/Faith	Protection, power, initiative
Second ray	Jophiel/Christine	Illumination, perception, wisdom
Third ray	Chamuel/Charity	Love, tolerance, gratitude
Fourth ray	Gabriel/Hope	Purity, resurrection, artistic development
Fifth ray	Raphael/Mother Mary	Healing, concentration, Mary truth, scientific development
Sixth ray	Uriel/Aurora	Devotional worship, ministration, peace
Seventh ray	Zadkiel/Amethyst	Ordered service, culture, refinement, diplomacy, invocation

As you can most likely gather from this, the archangels and the master chohans of the rays fall under the same basic energy structure [see chapter 2 for ray/chohan chart]. One important point to note, however, is that in recent times Saint Paul the Venetian and Serapis Bey have, in a sense, switched their primary ray with each other due to their overlapping work, as well as the need of the hour. Therefore, Serapis Bey now holds the primary energy as chohan of the third ray and Saint Paul the Venetian holds the primary energy of the fourth ray. These subtleties can seem a bit confusing, but I assure you that they make perfect sense on the inner realms where these types of decisions are made. Do not let yourself get bogged down over certain seeming discrepancies. Nothing remains stationary or static. Rest assured that if you have been invoking Serapis Bey with sincerity of intent and sincerity of heart, the appropriate response will come your way.

As long as I am on this subject, l will also point out another change of planetary office that seems to confuse many. If you are new to these teachings, then you would not fall among these, but if you do come across differing literature you can understand that changes have taken place among the governing forces of humanity and remember not to get hung up over these points.

This greater shift occurred during Wesak (Taurus full moon) 1995. During this time, Sanat Kumara, who held the office of Planetary Logos, moved on in his own evolution and was replaced by Lord Buddha. The jobs in the cosmos are as varied, if not infinitely more so, than those of Earth, so I ask you not to get confused by reading or hearing about these shifts. Stay within the appropriate energy flow and all your needs will be met. Whenever I hear of a new shift of position, it takes a bit of adjustment, but I realize that what seems like eternity from an earthly perspective is simply a moment within God's infinite time. I also recall that these beings, in changing job functions, do not have to worry about incomes, taxes or insurance. So if they move on unencumbered into their appropriate place, I simply allow myself to go with the flow, realizing that all discrepancies in this regard are simply *apparent* discrepancies, and that no prayer goes unanswered simply because I had thought I was sending it to one being rather than another.

The masters, logos, angels, archangels and the entire planetary and cosmic hierarchy respond to intent. I again tell you this because the angels and archangels are specifically attuned to the pure intent of heart. All truths presented here are truths that are most current. The greatest truth, however, lies within the heart of each of us, and it is there we reach the heights of our own spiritual beingness.

Bearing in mind the shifts of office that have recently occurred, I will again list for your convenience the master chohans associated with each ray so you can associate the appropriate archangels working with that ray.

First ray	Master chohan El Morya
Second ray	Master chohan Kuthumi
Third ray	Master chohan Serapis Bey
Fourth ray	Master chohan Paul the Venetian
Fifth ray	Master chohan Hilarion
Sixth ray	Master chohan Jesus/Sananda
Seventh ray	Master chohan St. Germain

As the above-mentioned masters and archangels work in constant cooperation with each other, it is advised that you call upon both the master of the ray and the archangel who works on that ray to help effectuate a specific purpose. However, this is not necessarily the way to go in all cases, since each plays a unique part within the same field of service. Asked who to call at any given time, I would tell you that you would be the best judge in these matters, as long as you follow your heart. Let your heart, mind and intuition work together, and know that the archangels and masters alike stand ever ready to serve.

The Angels

Under the direct influence of the archangels, whose function is to overlight large areas of service, are the more personal angels. Within this category fall groups of angels, such as the healing angels, angels of beauty and harmony, angels of peace, guardian angels of the home, angels of mercy, angels of ministry, angels of the garden and so forth.

On a still-more-personalized level is the guardian angel who accompanies an individual throughout his/her various incarnations. There is also an angel who best serves a person in any given incarnation and who works alongside the guardian angel. In a sense then, we each have one guardian angel, who is with us throughout our various incarnations, who knows us inside out and whose function it is to help and protect us on every level of our being. We likewise have the aid of an angel who is particularly attuned to who we are during any specific incarnation. This angel joins our guardian angel and helps in more specific ways. For example, if we are having a life involving harsh health lessons, we will have with us an angel particularly skilled in the healing arts. If we are in a particularly artistic lifetime, we will then have the added help of an angel who specializes in the arts.

The point I am trying to make is that the hierarchy of angels and archangels is a reality and that it is as practical as any reality readily perceived by the senses. So often we feel utterly bereft and alone. But truly we are never alone. Not only do we have the masters and our inner-plane lineage of specific masters to turn to, but we also have the hierarchy of angels, our own personal guardian angel who journeys with us throughout our incarnations, and the specific angel who serves us during any given lifetime.

In addition, we have the groups of angels to whom we may call whenever a particular need arises, such as Raphael and the entire ministry of healing angels or Lord Michael and the army of spiritual light warriors when we need protection. In each hospital and healing clinic and by every bedside are specific heralding angels, hovering, waiting eagerly to be called into service. Within each home are the guardian angels of the home, also awaiting invocation.

You can help them be of service to you by calling upon them. Don't simply wait until a time of crisis to call them forth; learn how to invoke their activation within your daily life. The angels actually evolve through serving humanity. Our two lines of evolution are not mutually exclusive but interrelated and interdependent.

One delightful way to honor your guardian angels and all members of that evolutionary sphere is to create an altar specifically for that purpose. As all the angels are drawn to beauty and love, the altar can be simple, yet designed beautifully, harmoniously and lovingly. A picture or statue of an angel could be present. Add some fresh flowers and sweet-smelling incense. The design is entirely up to you. I suggest you spend a brief period each morning and evening at this little altar just giving thanks to the angels and the part they play within your life and the world in general. This will be most appreciated by them and will help strengthen the bond between you and your particular guardian angels. It will also strengthen the bond between you as a representative of humanity and the angelic kingdom as a whole. They will thank you by engulfing you in an outpouring of divine love, sharing their energy in a subtler fashion, or perhaps even in a vision. Whatever way they choose, they will give you the response best suited to you. So if you don't seem to feel anything, that doesn't mean they are not giving forth anything. Odds are, you will feel something quite wonderful. But, no matter what is or is not immediately felt, your honoring them will do a great service both to yourself and to their entire hierarchy.

Pan: The Overlighting Deva of the Nature Kingdom

In writing about the angels, Pan, the overlighting deva of the entire nature kingdom, cannot be overlooked. All nature spirits are under Pan's direct guidance, and he might be called the god of the nature spirits. His appearance is that of half-man, half-goat, which unfortunately has given him a bad reputation. In truth, he exists but to serve God. In fact, he is one of the devas, who, though functioning primarily in gardens, forests, meadows and every area where nature spirits are, can also be called upon to help heal human ailments. This is because, as overlighting deva for all nature spirits, those whose function it is to build the human form are also included within his sphere.

Since devas hold the archetypal plan and the nature spirits and elementals are the builders of that plan, this line of evolution is equally responsible for building not only the form of every carrot, pea, rose or entire garden, but the form of humanity as well. This is a vast subject, and shall not be undertaken in this material. It is, however, important to take note of, since Pan is now being invoked in the healing of human ills as much as in the healing and proper growing of a garden.

The Practicality of the Devic and Angelic Beings

The purpose of removing the angels from the realm of folklore, childhood fables and dancing on the head of a pin is extremely vital. The entire thrust of the ascension movement itself is the merger of heaven with earth and earth with heaven—a process of transformation and practicality. The positive effect of talking or singing to one's plants has now become household news. The housewife of two decades ago has become the home gardener of today, talking to and playing music to her plants, which thrive as never before. This has been well documented and covered by the media. If this, however, still seems like fantasy to you, then I advise you to check out the book *The Secret Life of Plants* and see what I am talking about. Or, better yet, try some experimentation yourself.

In the early '70s some remarkable occurrences happened in a small Scottish community named Findhorn. Living in a handful of caravans were a very special group of people who were in direct contact with the nature spirits, the overlighting devas of various plant kingdoms and with Pan himself. Following the guidance of these beings, they nurtured sandy soil of such poor quality it was deemed incapable of producing even the smallest vegetables. Yet they grew cabbages, broccoli and other vegetables of the same ilk as Jack's mythical beanstalk—of unprecedented size—truly fit for a kingdom of giants.

Should you want to investigate this community and their vegetable miracles yourself, I recommend reading *The Findhorn Garden* by the Findhorn community. In the '70s a documentary film was made about the Findhorn Bay community and their incredible gardens. I don't know if this video is still available, but it is worth trying to find. I likewise recommend trying to obtain a copy of *Behaving as if The God in All Life Mattered* by Machaelle Small Wright. Learning about the societies of the people of Findhorn and Perelandra as well as *The Secret Life of Plants,* should go far toward putting you in touch with the benefits of working with this glorious unseen world.

In Your Own Garden

The ultimate test of the practicality of this blessed kingdom lies, of course, with you. If you are fortunate enough to have a garden of your own, try working with the devas of that garden, as well as with the nature spirits and Pan himself. If you are growing house plants, you might as well start there. Try playing some soothing music to a withering plant, telling it you love it, giving it a name and asking for inner guidance on what is best to help it grow.

In the same way work with all angels at every level, for the angelic line of evolution has much to give. And it is in mutual cooperation that the human and angelic lives shall both evolve in glory. Ask the healing angels to work on the garden of your physical/etheric, astral/feeling and mental/thought bodies. Call upon the archangels and the various angelic groups and never forget that you have a guardian angel who knows you from a more intimate vantage point than even your own. Talk to your guardian angels and ask them for help. They will help, for that is who they are as well as what they do.

It is time for the two evolutions to work in mutual love, trust and cooperation with each other. At this point, it is humanity that must catch up with the work of the angelic hierarchy. We can do this if we allow ourselves to actually work with them. This is the time of Earth's great acceleration. The angels ask to be taken from the realm of speculation and fantasy and brought into the heart-life and practical life of all humankind. Let us give this a try by opening up our hearts and minds to ascension (another term for resurrection) and going into and merging within the light, love and power of God and the beloved angelic kingdom, which seeks to aid us at every turn.

The joy is in the reality of these hidden worlds, which are now beginning to emerge into the range of humanity's vision and this is a glorious thing indeed. I am not asking you to have faith here, but to experiment with the reality of these unseen mysteries to experience them for yourselves.

The Angelic/Human Interblending

Before closing this discussion, one more piece of this vast puzzle of cosmic unfoldment needs to be added. At certain times for specific purposes, under guidance of the archangels and planetary and cosmic masters, certain monads will be allowed to evolve and serve on the path between the winged and human ones. A merging and blending occurs where a soul, often of the angelic line, will take a certain number of human births (set forth by the joint decisions of the karmic board, that soul, the hierarchy of angels and humanity) to fulfill the purpose of carrying the essence of both lines of evolution. Please bear in mind that this is not the norm, although it certainly is an aspect of evolution that must be considered. Second, do not spend precious time away from your service or ascension work figuring where you fit into this picture. It is the work that is important, not the glamour of the work. If, by the unusual chance this applies to you, it will be made known to you if and when that knowledge serves the greater purpose.

Having said that, it is well you know that a path such as the blending of the winged and human ones does exist. These beings are among us, and usually have a history since childhood of extreme sensitivities to the harshness of the earth (although so does much of humanity who has progressed along the path of initiation). These half-winged-ones have usually been the target of many childhood jokes, often being referred to as sprites or elves and described as floating on a cloud, not here, space cadets and so forth. They always seem to carry a certain magical quality about them and might have been categorized as different or special. They have generally been quite misunderstood.

These childhood remarks actually pinpoint the truth that, indeed, they are not fully here in the general sense of that term. They are, however, most profoundly here to serve, bring and anchor the angelic presence within the wellsprings of humanity. Many of these beings have their point of origin closely associated with the planet Venus, since Venus gave much to the birthing of Earth's humanity in prehistoric times, helped greatly by both the angelic and advanced human souls. Sanat Kumara, who held the position of Earth Logos until 1995, was himself connected to Venus. This connection between Earth and her sister planet extends into this present period and shall go beyond it.

Some of the half-winged-ones have built much more human essence into their aura than others, spending a great deal of time studying with the ascended masters who evolved along the human line. Others have spent less time clothed in matter. Again, it all comes down to the specific service work agreed upon at the outset of this blend. It might be of interest to note that Merlin the Magician manifests himself as a blended one.

This likewise works in reverse. The human monad may blend much of itself into the devic or angelic line of evolution to serve that evolution in a similar but reverse pattern. Upon the highest levels, these hierarchies blend and merge in a way hard to comprehend from the three-dimensional point of view. The essence of this understanding should lead you, beloved readers, back to the core of all these teachings, which is unity in diversity and an ultimate sense of the oneness between all life.

I close this chapter with the prayer that the hierarchy of angels and the hierarchy of humanity live in the cooperation, interdependence and peaceful love that God intended. Amen.

10

Our Animal Brothers and Sisters

The Wild Animals

Let us consider the less-evolved of the animal species. These animals live in the wild, basically without any contact or interaction whatsoever with human beings. Evolutionarily speaking, these younger members of the animal kingdom are just awakening to the very basic, fundamental levels of their existence. They function primarily on instinct and develop through harsh contact with other animals of a similar development and through interaction with the primal environment about them.

They are basically made aware of their existence through intense hunger, the instinct to kill or be killed, intense but mindless fear and pain. These animals fall into the category of lower mammals, prehistoric reptiles, reptiles and certain fishes of the deep. (I include fish in this discussion although they are not animals, per se). Again, these animals have no contact with the human kingdom.

A bit further along the line are wild animals, but these have some form of interaction with the human species, even if it is just via scent or an occasional opportunity to prey upon a human being. Seemingly, there is no difference from the category that has absolutely no contact with human life, but just by virtue of coming into contact with the next level up the evolutionary process, some very subtle changes come about. These changes are minimal, but there is a slight lifting of the aura of the animal, simply by making contact with the human species. This difference is quite minute but I mention it to reveal a bit about the impact of human interaction, even at such a basic level.

The next step up for the animal involves human interaction. I am not speaking here of the domestic interaction we have with our pets, but rather the interaction that occurs in certain jungle areas where humans and animals live in close proximity to each other. There we find wild lions, tigers and so forth, but now they are coming across the path of man on a daily basis. Humanity affects these wild animals in a vibratory fashion, and they begin to form some type of response system to humankind. This occurs on a very subtle level, but the energies of humanity begin rudimentarily to have an impact upon the animal kingdom, thus adding a certain coloration to that of the animal group.

Out of this group of animals develops the wild animal who is adopted as a pet. People were known to have pet lions, tigers or wolves, and some still do. This begins to have a profound effect on the animal, as we shall see when we explore the esoteric process of evolution from animal to human being.

Our Pets and Domesticated Animals

The next grouping of animals comprises those we call our pets. Generally speaking, these are all the species of dog and cat, bird, horse, elephant, truly domesticated wolf, lion and so forth. The latter are exceptions to the rule, but do exist. I am speaking of wolves, lions and other animals so highly trained that they are well-paid actors in films. The bond between them and their handlers is very deep, although it does not approach the bond of the truly domesticated animal, except in rare cases with wolves.

It is important to keep in mind the closeness of the relationship between the animal member of a family and its owners (surrogate parent or pack), as we discuss the evolution of the animal soul journeying toward the human kingdom. At present, the doorway into the human kingdom is closed and has been since Atlantean times, except in extremely rare cases. This door will be opened again in a distant cycle or round of evolution. The animal ultimately evolves through human interaction and therefore pets play a great part in the evolutionary scheme. It is not we alone who think of them as part of the family. They, in turn, consider us truly to be their family, and for the average cat, dog, evolved horse and pet elephant, we are. I remind you that the Native Americans refer to the animals as their younger brothers and sisters, which is the way God would have us see it.

Emotions and Animals

An interesting attribute of the animal kingdom, and one that shall fit perfectly with the explanation of the evolution of this kingdom, is the part that they play within the emotional world. All animals are sensitive to emotions, even wild ones, and the karma of both the human and animal kingdoms are interconnected on that level. Wild animals take on the imbalance of massive group actions that were originally brought forth through the human kingdom, such as war, famine, poverty and mass death. Even the wildest of animals will help channel some of the negative reactions that we have brought upon ourselves.

To an even greater extent does the little family member whom we call pet channel this energy. Our pets do this for us in a variety of ways, including taking on the karma that we would have incurred.

The Evolution of the Animal Kingdom

The animal kingdom has not yet reached the point of individualization. Becoming individualized souls is in fact the next stage of development for this kingdom. This, then, is the very goal toward which they are moving. This is not to say that the animal kingdom is not vital to the flow of evolution in and of itself; only that just as all kingdoms are important to the whole, they are likewise moving forward upon the pathway of evolution.

Picture a glass of water. Imagine that glass to represent all the lions in existence everywhere upon the globe. Each time a lion takes an incarnation, it experiences things somewhat individually (there is always the herd aspect), yet remains linked to that one glass of water. When a lion dies, after a brief stay in the astral world, the essence of all that the lion experienced flows back into that single glass of water, or group soul. At this particular phase of an animal's development it forms part of a group soul without having developed an individualized soul.

Every single experience that that lion has adds to that single glass of water, changing it ever so slightly with its unique coloring. As time moves on and more lions incarnate, the glass of water becomes more reflective of the group experience of all the lions that ever existed. Much of the instinct of the lion is that of design and much of it is the result of the cumulative experience of the specific group soul to which it belongs.

This is now the basic pattern for most of the animal kingdom—they are busy building up their individual group-soul bodies, or filling their unique glasses of water. Interesting to note is how this functions in, for example, the deer, which are so cruelly hunted for sport. Although deer are docile and friendly by nature, their group soul has built up a cumulative, and I might add appropriate, fear response to mankind. Therefore, they shy away from people, as the inherent deer soul memory guides them away from anyone who might potentially be the hunter.

In the case of the dog, cat, horse or elephant, another piece of the puzzle is added. What begins with the glass of water that represents "dogness," after centuries of interaction with humanity, becomes separated into various species of dog.

The domesticated dog then begins a series of incarnations as a distinct personality. Although not truly individualized in the same sense that a person is, this specific entity is truly the same personality evolving life after life, singularly and not simply as part of a group soul. It adds to its separate reservoir of experiences its unique experience through various incarnations and differs from a person only in the principle of mind because the fully individualized causal and mental vehicles have not yet been brought forth. Thus a divine son/daughter of God as we know ourselves, has not yet come to be, but it could be looked at as a son or daughter of God on a slightly lower rung of evolution. Nevertheless, at this stage there is quite a distinct personality at play.

This baby human, as I affectionately call a domestic animal at this stage, can choose from various domesticated group energies the particular body and form in which it can best serve and further its evolution. Hence your pet lion from a previous incarnation in Egypt can be your kitty of today. Be mindful, however, that this choice and ability applies only to those animals who are having singular incarnations.

Factors Determining Individualization

The primary factor involved in the individualization process of a domesticated animal or pet is that of its interaction with its surrogate human family. Within that interaction, the energy that plays the largest part upon the development of the animal is the energy of love. The love flow between your pet and yourself plays a phenomenal part in developing your pet's astral/emotional nature. The more love flow between a pet and its family, the faster the animal will move toward its hour of individualization.

Animals are primarily connected with the heart center of the humans with whom they have contact, as well as with the divine overlighting energy or angelic forces that supervise the growth of the animal kingdom. This is not a theoretical fact, but something that all animal lovers experience for themselves.

The Psychological/Mind Connection Between Humans and Pets

Animals are also quite responsive to the mental atmosphere of humanity in general. To the people with whom they are closest, this takes on an even greater depth due to the deeper interaction between them. When an owner turns his/her mental attention upon her pet, speaking to it, explaining things to it, she stimulates the latent aspect of mind that has been dormant within that animal. The pet then begins to develop a rudimentary psychology, which is quite unique and specific to that particular animal.

Over the past twenty years there has been an enormous increase in the phenomenon of animal psychologists and even animal psychics. This might seem a bit outlandish to the less animal-attuned person, but presented in the proper light, can be easily seen as reality.

The uninitiated are likely to believe that animal psychics are anthropomorphizing when they claim to read the minds of their pets, but I assure you, they are not. True, the mind structure is not fully formed. However, the blueprint for that growth is there, and the development of their emotional bodies combined with the semblance of a thought world allow true psychic and psychological impressions to be picked up. The person of little experience with animals might relegate this to animal instinct but, in truth, it is animal evolution and progression. Very real, heightened emotional responses are involved, as well as the beginnings of psychological and mental acuity. Your pet is not *just* a dog or cat. They are, in fact, animal children, moving toward the process of individualization and ultimate human incarnation, and they should therefore be treated with more respect and sanctity than our modern-day society gives them.

Final Comment on Our Animal Brothers

All I have shared about humanity's interaction with the animal kingdom and its enormous effects will hopefully lead each of you to explore the reality of this for yourselves. It is my fervent hope, however, that you will take enough of this on faith and inner attunement to realize the importance of the tender handling of the animal kingdom.

Animals are part of the great chain of evolution and look to us for guidance in taking their next great leap forward. Humanity is responsible for nurturing the animal kingdom's development, just as the inner-plane ascended masters and the Spiritual Hierarchy are responsible for helping humanity develop. The domesticated animal has an extremely sensitive nature, although some are more emotionally sensitized than others, depending on their particular level of evolution and the path on which they are proceeding. Nevertheless, we humans function both as teacher and parent to these incredible beings, who rely on us for their very existence.

These delightful beings are no longer creatures of the wilderness. They are not the wild animals who are, in one very real sense, their younger brethren. They are much more like little children, dependent on humans for feeding them, stroking them, playing with them, interacting with them and providing them with the stimulation of love and communication that will propel them into their next phase of evolution.

Please treat them kindly, gently and with the respect they deserve. They are, after all, the representatives of our own pasts, even as we are the hope of their future. They are also the joy of the moment. And, if we have adopted one of these babies into our care, then let us give them the care we committed to by virtue of agreeing to parent their evolution.

11

Our Brothers and Sisters of the Stars
The Idea of Space Brethren

To some, the idea that we as a race and species are not alone in the universe seems like science fiction. Frankly, this attitude I find difficult to relate to, even in a most logical vein. Pure reason reveals such vast numbers of star systems, let alone the suns and the planets that revolve around them, that I cannot possibly conceive of humankind being alone in the universe. However, I am assuming that you, my beloved readers, range from those who equate life among the stars with science fiction to those who are avid believers, and this chapter is dedicated to all of you.

I do not try to convince anyone of anything, but simply to share the truth as I see it and leave it to the meditations of your own hearts, minds and intuitions to decide for yourselves what you believe. I do request, however, that you read this chapter as I've asked you to read all others, with an open mind and heart and a willingness to expand.

Some information, which I shall touch on only lightly, I have devoted half of my book *Hidden Mysteries* to. It is an in-depth exploration of extraterrestrial beings, using the best available literature on the subject, as well as my own personal experience and understanding. I shall not indulge in too much repetition here; however, there cannot help but be a bit of overlap when exploring a subject of this nature.

The main thrust of introducing this concept to you is twofold. First, to those of you who are not familiar with these beings from the outer reaches of space, I would like to introduce to you. As with all subject matter in this book, you will see how our own evolution as a race is interdependent and ultimately connected to that of other worlds.

Second, for those of you who are familiar with certain aspects of Earth's interactions with beings from other planets, solar systems and galaxies, it is important that you know that most of these beings are of benign intent, and they function here in accordance with the will of God.

There is so much confusion about this, so much misunderstanding. While it is true that some of the beings have come to our planet with strictly selfish purposes, this is the exception rather than the rule. Film, television and the media seek to play upon our fears in this matter. This likewise has a dual purpose. One, it keeps us fearful, and being fearful we will avoid trying to push through the veil that some governments of the underworld have created. Also, by keeping us in fear, these governmental powers can continue to control us, because fear makes us vulnerable.

I seek to shift your viewpoint from one of doubt and fear to one of awe and amazement, joy and celebration that the unity of all life is indeed the unity of *all* life. Furthermore, I hope to broaden your perspective to see that life and is not confined to the life of our specific planet, solar system, galaxy or even universe.

The Evolution of Humanity and Our Space Brethren

From the very beginning of Earth's evolution, particularly from the point when infant humanity began to use it as a schoolhouse upon which to evolve, more highly evolved beings from other worlds and star systems came to aid us in our development. These beings are often referred to as *sons of fire* since one of their primary functions was to stimulate the newly activated aspect of mind in infant humanity.

One of the most influential beings in the development of man upon Earth is Sanat Kumara, who, functioned as Planetary Logos for Earth until as recently as 1995. This great being came with a host of others from the planet Venus, which is known in occult literature as the sister planet to Earth. As Planetary Logos, Sanat Kumara functioned in his highest aspect as "he who held the Earth within his aura and all that was contained therein." Beside him worked several extremely advanced beings who interacted with humanity to guide its mental and moral development.

At the dawning of Earth's history, even as there are today, there were a vast number of so-called extraterrestrials, whose primary function was aiding the development of humanity. Whereas during our early stages as a species, the primary function of these beings was to aid us in developing the principle of mind and to help structure civilization itself. How the intent of the positive extraterrestrial influence is to help our evolutionary step into the fifth, or spiritual kingdom. They are also here to help save us from ourselves, so to speak, and to guide us in developing our higher faculties. These positive extraterrestrials post guard over the few negative groups, keeping them at bay to the best of their ability, without interfering in human free will. Unfortunately, there are members of our government who have chosen to join forces with some of the less-than-positive groups.

The basic motivation for this is greed, desire for power and control. All the positive groups can do is to work with those of us who open to their positive influence. They cannot interfere with the negative choices some of humanity makes. That is why it is up to people of good will to manifest that goodness whenever and however possible.

Some of the most helpful of this type of space brother/sisterhood are the Arcturians, Commander Ashtar and the Ashtar Command, the Pleiadians and the Venusians, to name a few. They each have specific purposes in being here, all of which are related to the service of humanity from a higher spiritual consciousness. The Venusians have been with the Earth since its inception. Their work now is specifically to help us achieve the level of true brotherhood that they have achieved and to impart to us more of their pure love essence.

Why We Don't Often See the ETs

Many beings working with us have evolved to such a high degree that the physical matter of their bodies is of a much more refined structure. The best way to understand this is to visualize them as functioning at a vibrational frequency much like those beings from the nature kingdom discussed in the previous chapter. Both these evolutionary lines are in physical manifestation. The difference between us and them is that they are functioning more in the etheric realm.

The etheric realm is closely tied to the physical, as I explained earlier. It is the physical functioning at a faster and higher rate of frequency that generally renders them invisible to the human eye. For this reason, the scientific community holds the belief that there is no life on the planet Venus. This is absolutely not the case. What is true, however, is that members of the Venusian race have developed to such a refined degree that their physical existence has been elevated to the etheric realm. The planet now holds a vital place in the physical cosmology of the universe, although it no longer serves as "home" for the physical Venusian population. This does not mean that her physical structure is obsolete in the greater scheme of things, but simply that to the third-dimensional eye the planet *appears* to house no life forms.

Many are opening up to fourth- and fifth-dimensional seeing, and the Venusian race, as well as most of the benevolent ETs and fairy folk, are coming into the range of our seeing. I point this out lest your concrete minds try to discard the vast realm of beings that are and have ever been part of Earth's evolution simply because they do not fall within the range of normal seeing. If this concept seems far fetched, consider how limited the world appears to the extremely myopic individual. Consider the limited spectrum of an individual who cannot read without glasses. Seeing into the other worlds is akin to putting on the lens of etheric seeing, and it's a lens that is rapidly being made available to an increasing number of people.

The Arcturians

As far as extraterrestrial civilization is concerned, the Arcturians, headed by the Lord of Arcturus, are the most God-focused and God-realized beings in our galaxy. Their basic philosophy and teaching is that of love itself, and all forms of negativity, fear, guilt and separative thinking have no place at all.

Like the Ashtar Command, they encircle the Earth with advanced spacecraft that offset interference from warlike, negative ETs and, in fact, have kept us out of harm's way many times, averting disaster before it had the chance to enter into our sphere. That they would protect us in such a fashion is actually not surprising since they believe all life forms are their brothers and sisters, and they have both the heart and the advanced technology to do this. They stand as protectors of all evolving life within the universe and work directly with humanity itself to help it elevate its collective consciousness into the fifth, or spiritual kingdom, as quickly and as safely as possible.

They have bases in every country on our planet, using the dream state to heal and revitalize. At times they appear to people physically, but more frequently they communicate with humanity via telepathy or channeling. Through their refined and subtle-healing technologies, I have been helped by them many times, simply by requesting assistance from the Lord of Arcturus and the Arcturians. In like manner my light quotient has been raised and my body energized, as well as being enabled to work with an increase of energy.

They work, as do the inner-plane ascended masters, to help in all ways possible to uplift humanity to a closer attunement with God. Like the ascended masters, they will not interfere with humanity's free will and they wait to be called upon to serve. Because their intent is totally aligned with the intent of God and the good, I suggest you avail yourself of their services by inviting them to help you in your daily life and as you continue on your journey toward God realization.

The Pleiadians

The Pleiadian civilization is another wonderful, advanced ET race but the particular characteristics vary a bit as to what Pleiadian group one is communicating with. Also devoted to service and uplifting humanity, they view humans as their brothers and sisters within the divine spiritual family, which includes the universe. They come from a star cluster in the constellation Taurus, which lies approximately five hundred light-years from Earth.

The Pleiadian race is one of the most advanced in this galaxy in terms of music and dance, which would indicate a strong fourth-ray influence. They are subtly bringing this music through inspired music channelers on Earth. The effect of this will raise vibrational frequencies of all who listen to it, for this is an aspect of the music of the spheres. They also will stimulate great advancements in the use of light, holograms and laser technology.

In coming here, they seek to enlighten humanity by showing us that we are not alone and that many benign forces have come to aid us in the ways most appropriate to their specific civilizations. They do caution us about the negative ETs, so that we are aware of them and alert to their strictly selfish intent. Their main purpose is, again, to help us better align with God and the will of the Creator.

The Sirians

The system of Sirius has a very direct link with Earth and our solar system. The Sirians have been among us since the time of the Mayan and Egyptian civilizations and were responsible for the building of the great pyramids. Just as they were active in earlier times, so will they be active in helping humanity usher in the golden age yet to come. At present, their work with humanity is less interactive than it was in the past or will be in the future, although they are helping in subtle ways.

The extraterrestrial civilization of Sirius is different from the inner-plane Sirius, known as the Great White Lodge. Shamballa, the inner-plane capital of Earth and home of Lord Buddha, our Planetary Logos, is just an outpost under the leadership of the Lord of Sirius.

The Hollow Earth

There are, in fact, many advanced extraterrestrial cultures living in cities inside of the hollow Earth. In *Hidden Mysteries*, and in Earlyne Chaney's writings, we give detailed accounts of advanced physical human beings in the past and now living in the center of the Earth, as well as underground cities all over the planet. This might seem like science fiction to many, however, I assure you it is not. In both Chaney's and my writings we confirm the fact that Earth has an inner sun and an opening at both ends of the poles. This has actually been discovered by the United States government. However, it has been kept secret, as all the extraterrestrial information has. The United States government has more than one hundred physical bodies of aliens who have died in UFO crashes, as well as twenty to thirty UFO aircraft they are experimenting with.

If we trace the ancient writings of Native Americans, particularly the Pueblo Indians, Chinese, Egyptian and Eskimo peoples, we will find common the belief that a race of people live beneath the Earth in hidden cities. These are not all of an extraterrestrial nature, since some of them are products of Earth evolution, but they are evolving within the womb of the Earth rather than upon its surface.

The Negative Extraterrestrials

The type of extraterrestrials we are most familiar with, unfortunately, is what I call the negative extraterrestrials. We are most aware of them because the media, ever in search of the sensational, has decided to entertain us by indulging our fears of the unknown and presenting to us only the darker side of a truth that is mostly composed of light.

Nevertheless, it is worth our paying heed to the fact that the group termed the Grays, as well as a reptilian-type race (among a few others) do not have our best interest in mind. These beings are operating through the negative ego, acting selfishly and abusing humanity for their own purposes. These are the beings responsible for the abusive abductee scenarios. It is actually positive that we are aware of their presence here on Earth, for with knowledge there is the power and ability to change things!

These beings are the ones infamous for implanting those whom they choose to track. On subtler levels, they can implant (and this they have done to almost the entire human population) via etheric and astral means. Fortunately, certain advanced initiates now have the ability to remove these implants through spiritual means, as well as the knowledge of how to deactivate them. I suggest a clearing be done on everyone, for everyone has them to one degree or another. We have for the most part been functioning fine with them, so please do not let the element of fear about this creep into your consciousness. By the same token, however, we can function better without them. If you would like a trained professional to help clear negative implants, call me at the number in the back of this book and I will recommend someone to you. If you notice blockages in certain areas of your life that don't seem to fit or if you have recollection of an abduction, it is a good idea to have a professional help you get started. You can then continue the program yourself on an ongoing basis.

Preventive Protection from Negative ETs

There is no need to become fearful regarding these beings, for if you cultivate an attitude of spiritual centeredness, prayer and Christ consciousness and concentrate on building your light and love quotients, neither they nor any negative force can break through your armor of God. Oneness with the One, psychological integration, a loving and serving attitude and a mind held steady in the light are the supreme protection against all influences that are not of the highest will of God. This is ultimately the best tool that you can use in all circumstances and situations in your life, as well as calling upon the planetary and cosmic masters, some of whom have become masters through evolution upon other worlds and in other star systems. One of the basic tenets of the path of ascension and spiritual growth is that we are masters not victims. I want to make it one hundred-percent clear here that this applies to negative ET activity and alien abduction. Take a firm stance within your conscious mind and within your prayer life that this is unacceptable, and this will be the truth of your reality. Never let it be forgotten that you are a cocreator with God.

The Ashtar Command

One of the great protectors of the Earth, as well as other planets, is the Ashtar Command. They are a group of positive extraterrestrials who serve as a military deploy in the spaces above our planet. They have averted many potential interferences from negative races, holding them at bay and ultimately directing them away from the Earth while still remaining in what we would call the outer reaches of space. One finds it hard not to draw parallels between them and the ships of Star Trek, for they function in a similar fashion, being part of the unified Federation of Planets, which is a science fact rather than fiction.

Like the Federation in Star Trek, neither they nor any other positive ETs can infringe upon human free will. For this reason the Ashtar Command is more successful in diverting trouble from coming to our planet than in correcting already existing situations. I am referring to specifically the influence of the Grays. One of the main reasons they are allowed to do what they are doing via implants, abductions, mind control, experimentation and tracking is because an aspect of our government called the Secret Government has a subversive agreement with them.

When they first appeared here it was governmental leaders whom they sought out, striking a bargain to carry on their experimentation in exchange for providing our government with certain scientific information. The Grays have not kept their part of the bargain. Nevertheless, their influence and meddling continue. Since it was by the free choice of a group of humanity that the deal was made, neither the Ashtar Command nor the other races who aid us can do much about it. What they can do, however, is work to help us elevate our spiritual consciousness to a point where we become invulnerable to the Grays or any other negative influences in our lives. They are most dedicated to doing this, and, as I said before, work side by side with the ascended masters of our planetary and solar system, as well as those of other advanced civilizations. Therefore, what holds true here holds true in every regard. Center yourself always in your higher self and invite all that is of good and of God to help you achieve your own self-mastery. The more quickly each of us takes full responsibility for our own ascension, the more quickly the planet as a whole will function in the true unity and beingness of God, which is its ultimate destiny.

Conclusion

The point I make is simply that life is far vaster than even our imaginations. As we follow the path of initiation/ascension, it bodes well for us to likewise expand our view of that whole. That is why I have introduced you to our brothers and sisters from other worlds and likewise they who dwell within the Earth. My beloved readers, the oneness that we are expanding into is vast indeed. Do read *Hidden Mysteries*, for it is a comprehensive overview of the entire extraterrestrial movement and contains information about not only the inner spiritual worlds, but also the amazing things that are going on in our physical universe.

I have tried in this chapter to introduce you to a subject so vast as to warrant not simply one book, but countless books on the subject. My main purpose is to make you aware that there is much more good out there than negativity. Most of you are familiar with stories about abductions, but those who are newly becoming aware of the spiritual side of life are generally not acquainted with those wonderful races of star people who work with us, functioning as an extension of the brotherhood of light, love and power—the Hierarchy of masters to whom I introduced you in the beginning of this book.

Even those of you who are quite well-versed on the subject of extraterrestrial life could do well to focus, on ever-deeper levels, on the tools that are being made available to facilitate our healing and God attunement. Please consider calling upon the ETs as you do the inner-plane ascended masters, for in truth there is only one great brotherhood of God, and that includes all races and beings who function in oneness with the One of which we are all part.

12

The Many Lenses of Ascension
Ascension as Living

The process of ascension and initiation is the process of your daily life. Far too many people look at the process of initiation as one aspect of their lives and everything else as another aspect. This type of thinking is fragmented and runs counter to the goal of integrating initiation, ascension, meditation and spiritual development as a whole with the totality of one's beingness.

Being upon the conscious path of ascension and initiation does not mean that you stop being who you are. It means that you develop more fully and completely into the very best, or most spiritually attuned aspect, of who you are and then bring that fuller aspect into manifestation within the very life that you are living within your mental, emotional, physical bodies and environment.

Whatever your worldly profession, religion, personal preferences, tastes and so forth, you bring them right along with you into your transformative process. There will come a time when certain friends will fall away, tastes in music and other entertainment might go through transition and dietary habits will give way to healthier nutrition; however, the essential *you* will remain throughout. The real transformation will be in fine-tuning yourself to your best possible potential. What is truly needed is a disciplined and balanced approach to life on every level of your being.

The Lens of Light

The most common lens with which humanity looks at ascension is the lens of light. As we evolve, one important aspect of our initiatory work is to build our light quotients, that is, bringing greater frequencies of living light to fill every cell of all our bodies. This serves to anchor one of the most important attributes of God on Earth, which is light.

When we bring the light of God into the vehicles of our four lower bodies, we actually begin to raise the frequency of each of these bodies to higher levels. Thus, we move through the various sublevels of the physical, etheric, astral and mental bodies until we are functioning at the highest possible sublevel of each of them. Remember, these levels are interpenetrating and not stacked one above the other. In essence, this means that the higher we go, the more inclusive we actually become, since the levels are overlapping aspects of each plane. That which is higher or greater includes that which is lower or more limited and it is a process of expansion rather than one of exclusion.

Many lightworkers often seek to circumvent certain levels if they find they are not comfortable dealing with the lessons of that particular level or body. This, ultimately, will not work. There is no true ascension without integration, and each and every step must be mastered and appropriately addressed to free ourselves from the dictates of that particular level. Beloved readers, there are no shortcuts on the path of ascension and you will ultimately save yourself much trouble if you proceed slowly, step by step along your given pathway.

The Lens of Love

The lens of love must take its rightful place beside, and infused with, the lens of light. Complete ascension cannot exist without the blending of these two aspects. Much emphasis has been placed on infusing light within one's aura and four-body system (which includes and transcends the four lower bodies, since this includes the spiritual bodies, and this is appropriate. However, one cannot truly achieve the perfection he/she seeks without integrating the divine attribute of love.

This love is not the sentimental love of the poet, the dreamer, the lover or even the worshiper—although the latter comes the closest to what I am addressing. The love I speak of is the core essence of love itself. It is the embodiment of that principle divine that does not simply make the world go round, but *is* the very world and energy field in which we live, move and have our being.

We spoke earlier of the seven rays functioning in our planetary and solar systems. Of these seven rays, love/wisdom is the one governing our own solar system, and therefore it is intrinsic to our very nature. Looked at esoterically, love is a fact, not a fancy, and an aspect that must be fully incorporated into every cell of our four-body system in exactly the same way that light must be incorporated. The same general rule applies to moving through the sublevels of our bodies, integrating each with greater love frequencies in the same manner in which we moved through them with light.

Psychological Wisdom and Service

Just as love and light must function as one, so must wisdom (another aspect of light) and service (the inevitable outpouring and outpicturing of love). If we do not do this, then both love and light remain in the realm of the abstract and are not doing us much earthly good.

Psychological wisdom brings with it clarity of action and purity of intent. It allows for the light to be called into service by revealing the true nature of ourselves and our world, giving us the clarity of mind with which we can integrate, cleanse and heal that which needs it. It takes light from the vague and nebulous strata and allows it to shine upon our Earth, revealing hidden fragmentations and cleavages. This allows the needed adjustments to be made so that life and humanity, as part of it, function as fully integrated, balanced and whole beings.

Many of us enjoy being blinded by the light to the extent that much of what must be tended to is by-passed. This is all right for a temporary period since, it is natural for one to need to grow accustomed to brighter intensities of light. It, however, is not all right on a permanent basis, and far too many of us think we can remain blinded by the light and ignore the realities around and within us that seek to be revealed.

Ultimately, we will all be called to pay attention to the wisdom of the light and to straighten out our psychological selves. This applies to each of us individually, as well as to our whole planet.

Service is love made manifest. Without implementing service work into our ascension path, we are not allowing the love we have integrated within ourselves to be integrated within the world. As long as we refrain from giving love the expression that it seeks, we hold ourselves back from one of the most fundamental purposes of initiation and ascension.

As we ascend, we are rising up into ever-greater wholes. We are coming to terms in joy with our own unity with All That Is. If we are truly making progress upon this path, we cannot help but seek to serve. For we know that by serving others we are serving ourselves and God. Knowing ourselves to be one with the One, we realize that by helping others we are helping ourselves. For we are all part and parcel of the one essence of life—the I Am that I am.

Therefore, my beloved readers, I would thus far explain ascension as the integration and synthesis of the divine frequencies of love and light within the four-body system, manifesting in psychological healing of all fragments and cleavages within ourselves and our world through service to the One by the service of the many that constitute the One. There are, however, a few more aspects that must yet be integrated to present an accurate picture of ascension. Before I do that I share this statement on service by Lord Sai Baba, "Hands that help are holier than lips that pray."

Transcendence From Negative Ego to Christ Consciousness

Two areas that must ultimately be addressed to fully grasp the realization of ascension are negative ego, which sees via the separate self and Christ consciousness, which sees all in terms of the whole. Operating from negative ego includes thinking, perceiving and acting through the lens of selfishness, separation, greed, lust, manipulation, negativity, anger and fear. During the process of ascension, the thought process must be transferred from that of negative ego to that of Christ/Buddha consciousness.

There are really only two basic ways in which we can function: one, from negative ego and the other, from the higher Christ/Buddha consciousness. The former begets an attitude of separateness and selfishness, creating an entire behavioral structure built upon a faulty foundation. The latter springs from the fount of oneness, and outpictures in loving service to self and to humanity. Those who view the world and ourselves through the lens of the Christ mind, or spiritual consciousness, see it in terms of oneness, wholeness and love. These two consciousnesses cannot coexist in one who wants to realize God and become a full-fledged ascended master, rather than a partial or kindergarten ascended master.

The sincere initiate works on exposing, via the light, every pattern of faulty negative-ego thinking, using the clarity of wisdom to wipe the slate of their mind clean of the destructive influence of the negative ego. In its stead, through the wondrous and healing quality of love and attitudinal healing, the sincere initiate works to put forth only Christ/buddhic consciousness, and from that state of perceiving, he/she then participates in serving self and humanity.

This, my beloved readers, is a process that demands much attention, which is why I have given you specific tools and guidelines to use in your work. The time spent clearing the negative ego and reprogramming both the conscious and subconscious mind with the quality of Christ/buddhic consciousness will be well worth your while, and the rewards of peace, joy, love, unity, health, wholeness, oneness and liberation that await you will transform you into the truly spiritual being that you, and all of us, really are.

Synthesis/Mahatma Consciousness

Truly, ascension is the synthesized and balanced integration of light, love, psychological wisdom (leading to the transcendence of the negative ego) and service (which finds the natural expression by living within the realm of Christ consciousness). This process frees one from the wheel of rebirth and frees the initiate-turned-master to function from the higher planes downward rather than as the aspiring seeker looking upward.

I am speaking here of integrative ascension, which does not bypass nor deny any level of your beingness, but rather synthesizes and ascends all four bodies equally into the spiritual or monadic self. Through the process of integrated ascension you then become the perfect unique manifestation of God, able to fulfill your divine puzzle piece without the interference of your negative ego and with the full integration of all the divine qualities within you. With the negative ego transcended, the emotional body becomes spiritualized and positive, the mental body filled with divine wisdom and the physical body purified, healthy and filled with light.

The fact that a synthesized approach to integrated ascension will free you from the necessity to reincarnate upon the four lower worlds (physical, etheric, astral, mental) is true indeed. Likewise, is it true that as a fully integrated ascended being you will have vast potential both to express and to serve upon these lower worlds, and in joy you will be living out the wisdom and grace spoken of by beloved master Jesus when he told his disciples to be in the world but not of it. These worlds will become to you realms of experimentation and service rather than the enforced school of endless lessons and experience that they were before you achieved the status of the integrated and fully realized ascended master.

Therefore, while remaining in incarnation as an ascended being, you will not be leaving your life behind, but expanding it to include the divine. Ascension goes hand and hand with descension. Therefore, as you bring your Earth-self unto heaven, so do you bring and anchor your heavenly self upon the Earth.

Ascension and initiation, my beloved readers, is the most practical path anyone can travel. Whatever name you choose for this process, know that it falls under the banner of synthesis and is therefore the most complete and balanced approach to life for which one can possibly strive. It is a path that, in its truest and most complete sense, incorporates life as a whole—from the densest material Earth plane to the most refined spiritual planes. What it is not is a path relegated to the impractical dreamer. Being all inclusive, the true initiate seeks to give substance and manifestation to his/her loftiest dreams and visions, as well as to apply in a practical manner all that has been assimilated from the higher spheres.

It is important that you look at this path in this balanced and integrated light, with the full knowledge that ascension is not meant to separate you from the world but simply to give you life more abundantly.

13

Synthesis and Integration
The Synthesis Ashram

The synthesis ashram (or teaching center) is the place where synthesis takes form and substance and finds a direct point of communion between the inner and outer worlds. The manifestation of synthesis lies within the domain of the synthesis ashram, which is under the direct guidance of Djwhal Khul, master of the inner-plane synthesis ashram. This series of books also is being written under his guidance. Although this entire series is coming from Djwhal Khul's second-ray inner-plane ashram, the nature of the term "synthesis" means that all the inner-plane planetary and cosmic ascended masters are contributing to create a full-spectrum/full-prism lens in the *Easy-to-Read Encyclopedia of The Spiritual Path*. The goal is to provide an easy-to-read, practical, yet totally comprehensive set of books that provide the reader with all the information and tools to easily realize his/her ascension and seven levels of initiation in this lifetime.

Each of the ascended masters, or chohans, who are the leaders of the seven rays, or streams of energy, has an inner-plane ashram. The nature of each ashram will vary according to the way each particular master works, but teachings are offered on all the rays. Many of you might be familiar with certain ashrams on Earth. These are generally communities set up under the guidance of a particular master for the purpose of study and retreat. Two outer-plane ashrams with which many are familiar are the Self-Realization Fellowship, started by Paramahansa Yogananda during his earthly sojourn, and the ashram of Sathya Sai Baba, located in a remote part of India. Operating on different levels there are all sorts of ashrams where people go to meditate, study and connect with a particular guru or master.

The higher aspects of these ashrams are found on the inner planes. Some are run by very advanced masters. The ashram to which I am most connected, as are those who work closely with me, is that of the master Djwhal Khul. What makes his ashram unique is that it functions as a synthesis for the many ashrams and it is one to which students of all the ashrams go to study.

To get a bit more esoteric, there are four tiers to this ashram. From highest in rank to lowest, they are Lord Melchizedek, Lord Maitreya, masters Kuthumi and Djwhal Khul. This might be visualized as a four-story building on the inner plane. There are other ashrams connected with the head of each of the seven rays. However, the second-ray ashram is unique in the fact that Djwhal Khul's synthesis ashram is the only one that synthesizes all seven rays. And thus this series of books integrates all the ascended masters, all religions, spiritual paths, mystery schools and spiritual teachings. These are all overlighted by a cosmic being known as the avatar of synthesis and called the Mahatma. He is known as the avatar of synthesis because contained within his being are all 352 levels of being up to the very godhead itself. The Mahatma then brings forward not only the planetary understanding of synthesis, but the entire cosmic understanding of synthesis throughout God's infinite universe.

I speak of this to you, my beloved readers, because the idea of synthesis must now become a reality upon the Earth plane. The time of living in a place of separateness and division has passed. What is needed at every level is integration and synthesis, and this includes the affairs of the Earth as well as those more subtle aspects of self and the universe. That is why no matter what path a person is on or who his/her particular master might be, *all* must pass through the synthesis ashram on the inner planes to incorporate this important realization into their lives.

It is actually fairly easy to link with the synthesis ashram during meditation or sleep. Simply ask to be taken there in your bodies of light, or your spiritual bodies. There is much healing available in this most wonderful place, and it is there for the asking. There is a program available for the removal of fear—one of humanity's most difficult areas. I've addressed this program in *Beyond Ascension*, so I will not go into detail here. I will give you, however, the basics.

The Fear-Matrix-Removal Program

Call to Djwhal Khul, or any master with whom you feel closely aligned, and ask for help eliminating your core fear through the fear-matrix-removal program. Visualize the essence of your core fear and the specific form that fear takes in your life. Then visualize the master pulling that fear out of you like the pulling up of black roots. See them casting it into the all-consuming fire of God, transmuting all fear energies into pure energy, thus making it available to use for higher purposes. See the all-consuming fire of God dissolving this core fear. And then thank the particular master whom you have called. (Djwhal Khul is particularly adept at working this way, which is why I mentioned him first.) Finally, make a conscious effort to replace fear thoughts with love thoughts. Do this fear-matrix-removal program as often as you feel moved to, while simultaneously rebuilding your emotional and thought bodies upon the principle that "perfect love casts out all fear." The results of this program are wonderful, as many people will attest. Try it as on an ongoing process and see for yourself.

More on the Synthesis Ashram

Tuning in to the synthesis ashram will likewise tune you in to the masters with whom it is your destiny to work because all pass through this ashram during a phase of their initiatory process, and therefore all the masters have a definite connection to it. My guess is you who are reading this book are already familiar with the synthesis ashram upon the inner planes. That's why one of my goals is to open your conscious awareness to that which your higher awareness is already attuned. I suggest that you explore this ashram and its teachings during meditative periods designed exclusively with this goal in mind. You might have a notebook and pen on hand to see what comes through you in the form of journal-writing. You might find yourself pleasantly surprised that you are writing from your higher self on the causal/buddhic realm and bringing through much inspiration and guidance. Remember, synthesis and integration is the goal for Earth herself, so it is therefore the goal for each of us. And there is no better place to tune in to this aspect than within the synthesis ashram itself.

One last insight I would like to share about the synthesis ashram is that the four tiers of Djwhal Khul, Kuthumi, Lord Maitreya and Melchizedek is of second-ray lineage. The second ray in God's divine plan has to do with the spiritual education of planet Earth and ultimately the cosmos itself. The first ray deals with politics, the third ray with economics, the fourth with the arts, the fifth with science, the sixth with religion and the seventh with business. So it is out of the synthesis ashram of Djwhal Khul and the higher ashrams of Kuthumi, Lord Maitreya and Melchizedek that the unfolding revelation for the spiritual education of humanity is coming. And this set of books, as well as related teachings and workshops, are a part of this overall second-ray divine plan.

The Unity of Spiritual Paths and Religions

Although the unity between spiritual paths and various religions has been mentioned in passing, this matter requires deeper exploration. Humanity as a whole has been functioning with the attitude of segregation

between the many occult paths and, most certainly, between different religious paths. This has no place where ascension and taking initiations is
concerned. The process of initiation belongs to humanity as a whole, and
we must all be willing to fully embrace that fact to work together for the
benefit of all humankind—indeed, all kingdoms evolving upon this planet
and beyond.

The phrase "unity in diversity" has been used a lot lately, but it does
express a great cosmic truth. This is easiest to see when looking at the vast
array of individuals who constitute humanity. We are each
unique—physically, etherically, emotionally and mentally. This is apparent to all. What is often not honored is that we are essentially the same in
our human needs, from the simplest to the most complex. We are all *Adam
Kadmon*, an occult term for the prototype of humanity—made in the image
of God.

Our basic needs for food, love, security, shelter/home, purpose in our
lives and so forth are the basic needs of all of us. Our paths and approaches to meet these needs, however, might vary considerably according
to our specific culture, climate and level of initiation.

Across the Great Divide of World Religions

Many of us, particularly before taking the more mystical approaches
toward our involvement in our initiation process, adhere to the particular
religious affiliation into which we were born. There is nothing wrong in
this, since each religion is a particular lens through which to view and approach God, and it can be a very useful tool. In fact, if you conducted an
in-depth study of world religions, you would find that the same basic
truths pervade almost all of them, and that there is simply a differing approach toward the same end.

Another similarity is that most religions have revelations given in
graded successions to bring humanity one step further along the path of
evolution. I cannot help but look at the Judeo-Christian religions as two
parts of the same whole. I realize, however, that where there is total harmony of purpose for my colleagues and fellow initiates, there is a great
chasm dividing one segment of humanity from another.

One of the Hierarchy's primary goals is to heal the cleavages that
separate. In this healing, however, lies not the invalidating of one religion
and the validation of another, but rather the willingness of humanity to receive the best that each has to offer without denying anyone's own personal heritage. For example, there are many esoteric teachings within the
Jewish path that are only now becoming available to the general public.
The wonderful mysteries revealed in the Kabbalistic teachings are an example. These deeply spiritual teachings until fairly recently were

available only to the select few of the Jewish faith. Basically, only males over a certain age who were particularly studied had access to them. In exploring of these wonderful teachings I have found many parallels to the esoteric revelations of a variety of religions and spiritual paths.

My personal approach is quite eclectically universalistic, embracing all spiritual paths and religions. Included in this is my love and devotion to Jesus, Krishna, Lord Buddha, Rama, Mohammed, Confucius and the Virgin Mary, among others. All are but spokes on the great wheel of religious revelation, and each makes a valid contribution to the whole.

I truly believe the Judeo-Christian religions sprouted from the very same vine. The revelations brought forth through Jesus Christ (or Sananda via Lord Maitreya) is the further sprouting of tenets given through Moses and the prophets before Jesus. His birth was surely predicted in the Old Testament and viewed through a lens of inclusiveness. He himself was aware of it, since he said, "I have not come to destroy, but to fulfill the law of the prophets." I think, however, that this truth will take some time before it is rightly understood and embraced by both Jews and Christians alike.

If we opened our minds and hearts to the multifaceted aspects of all world religions, we would benefit from incorporating the vast amounts of wisdom, light and love contained therein. We would then perceive the truth made manifest by the beings who followed the path of spiritual leadership in the world and founded various facets of world religions during their successive incarnations. These powerful beings and masters had missions that were in the forefront of humanity's religions. In *The Ascended Masters Light the Way*, I explore this topic in great detail.

The Various Spiritual Paths

Those of you who are more eclectic by nature and desire active participation in your spiritual development have probably explored some of the Eastern or New Age approaches to the spiritual path. These have much to offer because by the nature of their design, they foster a desire to become a part of the process, rather than be relegated to a status of follower. When following some of these paths there remain pitfalls, however, if you segregate yourself from your brothers and sisters by thinking that you have found the one-and-only way. This would make you no different than the orthodox of any formal religion and you would inadvertently be creating a great divide of your own.

The purpose of the various paths should be to aid and inspire you on your own path of initiation. The path you choose to follow need not ever involve the terms "initiation" or "ascension" to indicate that this particular path or school of thought is aiding you along these lines. A wonderful example of this is the Self-Realization Fellowship. I personally have been a disciple of this path and made great strides in my initiatory process. This path does not involve much ascension terminology, but offers practical advice about daily living in the presence of God and a wonderful method of meditation. I have now come to the place within myself where I work exclusively with the inner-plane masters and meditate from the source of my inner connection to God, but if I felt that someone was particularly drawn to either the form of meditation that Self-Realization teaches or to its particular teachers, I would be happy to recommend this fellowship.

The same is true regarding his holiness, the Lord Sathya Sai Baba. I am a devotee of both him and his teachings, though I have never been to India. Nonetheless, my inner-plane communion with him has been, and continues to be, one of the greatest blessings of my life. By connecting with him in meditation and prayer, I have been healed, helped and uplifted beyond measure. I could go on about what I have learned through my prayers, devotions and meditations with Sai Baba. In fact, I have written a book dedicated to him, so I will not do that here. Anyone drawn to him should read *Golden Keys to Ascension and Healing: Cocreating with Sai Baba and the Ascended Masters* or find a Sai Baba center in his/her area. Or simply meditate upon him in the cave of your heart and see what arises for you.

I have likewise studied the teachings of Astara and the Theosophical Movement and the writings of Godfre Ray King in *The "I Am" Discourses*, Djwhal Khul through Alice Bailey and Vywamus and Djwhal Khul through Janet McClure. I bring forward these because they may be considered the first and second dispensation of ascended-master teachings. In my books I have tried to synthesize the best of all the teachings while also integrating the third, or new, revelation for the next millennium into one easy-to-read set of books.

The danger however, is the same that permeates the more traditional religions. When seen as separate rather than synthesized, these teachings create division and cleavages—the opposite of divine intent. Each unique path should be looked at as one of many bridges to help humanity cross into the realms of unity with God. These bridges, although adorned differently, are linked to the same Source—God, the One. On the path of initiation and ascension we might indeed call this divine energy the Father/Mother God, God the Father or the Divine Mother. Others might use the terms Brahma, Allah, nirvana, samadhi, oneness, self-realization and so forth. Ultimately, words fail anyway, so what a shame if we allow that which defies language to separate us one from the other. The ultimate truth is the same: from the One are we issued forth and to the One do we return. Therefore my prayer is that these wonderful and varied paths may be perceived as gifts from the One that may aid us on our path of return.

You might, if you share my temperament at all, find yourself first on one path and then upon another. Each pure path offers much, and it has been my personal inclination to get the best that each could offer me upon my own particular journey, and then move on. Ultimately, I have taken the best of all these worlds and incorporated/integrated them within myself, until I reached the point I am now at, which is simply to be the path myself. As I said before, I do not walk this path alone, but work daily and on a moment-by-moment basis with the inner-plane planetary and cosmic ascended masters. For me, this is the rocket ship method to God. All the diverse religions, spiritual paths, spiritual teachers and spiritual texts I now experience as one path, with the ascended-master teachings and connection being my foundation. After integrating all this within myself to the best of my abilities, the next step was to share this with you, my beloved readers, by writing these books with the ascended masters and, at times friends.

The Wesak Festival I put on for 1500 disciples and initiates every year at the full moon of Taurus is unique in that it is a gathering of lightworkers from all religions and spiritual paths. Gurus, spiritual teachers, spirit guides, starseeds and teachers from mystery schools and ashrams come together in total unity. To the ascended masters, this is the holiest day of the year and has been celebrated for eons on the inner plane. This is an opportunity for humanity to come together, restore and rejuvenate in spiritual fellowship with each other and the inner-plane ascended masters before another year of service and spiritual growth begins. Wesak, referred to as the Festival of the Buddha, holds great significance, especially since in 1995 Lord Buddha moved into the position of Planetary Logos, a position similar to president of planet Earth in the Spiritual Government. The Wesak celebration transcends all spiritual affiliations and forms of devotion and worship. If you are interested in attending the annual event, write or call for details, as well as other workshop, book and audio tape information (see back of book for number and address).

Across the Great Divide of the Races

Racial prejudice is an issue that has plagued humanity throughout history. There has always been the problem of one race subjugating another race, with the resultant response of either war or rebellion. The history of this particular problem is not one I shall detail here. The amount of literature extending from the earlier biblical era to today is massive. Unfortunately, all one has to do is turn on the television or radio, or in some cases, step outside the door, for the latest manifestation of this particular divide.

Viewed through the lens of the higher self and/or monad, this appears ludicrous. indeed. I have had experiences, when using the gift of higher-plane seeing, of perceiving people, everything for that matter, as pure energy rotating at various frequencies of light. For me, this magnificent experience pointed out how utterly incomprehensible the problems of racial prejudice are. This vision portrayed the cosmos itself as one vast whole, within which each of our individual selves formed miniuniverses. Even the idea of unity coexisting with diversity had a different meaning; for diversity lay within the realm and quality of vibrational frequency rather than apparent differences among people. As you might imagine, this vision and literally altered the way I looked at life from that point forward.

Without going into detail, I want to tell you that each of the races has a particular energy to contribute that is vital to the evolution of humanity as a whole. For example, the Eastern races (India, in particular) have exemplified the expression of the inner connection with spirit. Therefore, you also find a corresponding lack of development in outer-plane integration and expression, which is now beginning to seek a more balanced position. But the inner work of India is most apparent.

On the contrary, the occidental races (in America, for example) are typified by the outpicturing of form. Here what needs to be brought forth and integrated is the spiritual nature. This is also in the process of being balanced. One might be wise to pay attention to Native Americans, for they are unique in the demonstration of the unity between humanity and Mother Earth. An integral part of Native American culture involves a deep communion between self, nature and the animal kingdom—even to the point where the animal spirit is called on to provide guidance and assistance. Although much has been lost through ravaging this great culture through time, much has also remained. Humanity would fare well to learn from the essential teachings of these people to better integrate and cooperate with the forces inherent in nature, the various kingdoms and the Earth herself.

In a similar manner, each race has something unique and valuable to contribute, each adding its precious puzzle piece of divine unfoldment. One is not better than another, for each has its appropriate place.

It is man's mind alone that sees division where there is none. Differences, yes, but the great divide that humanity has constructed between the races comes from the faulty negative ego's interpretation, rather than from the spiritual or Christ mind. Individuals must now join together in the divine perception of the unity-within-diversity point of view. The Christ mind sees each person as the eternal self and as brother and sister, not as just a physical body with a certain skin color.

For those of you in integrated marriages, please know that there is great purpose within this melding of the races, as well. This is really not a new concept since throughout history men have found themselves on different shores, naturally resulting in marriages and children born of the blending of various races. As each race has much to offer in its uniqueness, so do those that result from the synthesizing of races. This allows offspring of such a union to hold within themselves the blended qualities of two or more races. The specific energies they can then express are those that come forth almost as a race itself, freeing an entirely new, expanded aspect of the whole to find expression. This is likewise part of the divine plan of God.

Let us all guard against the negative ego whispering its false ideas of separation, prejudice and segregation. Let us all see, hear and act from our higher selves, our Christ minds, so that what was once seen as a problem will be a cause for the celebration of unity in diversity.

Root Races

In occult wisdom, there is still another perspective where races are concerned: root races. Some races, in order of their development, include the following.

Lemurian race. Represented the process of individualization on Earth and the development of physical man, occurring approximately 10.5 million years ago. It focused on development of the first chakra and the very beginning of the second chakra. Hatha Yoga is the yoga for this root race.

Atlantean race. The root race in humanity's unfoldment, it focused on the development of the astral, emotional and psychic nature of humanity and on humankind's development of the second and third chakras. The yoga for this root race is Bhakti yoga.

Aryan Race. A still-existent root race in humanity's development, it focuses on mental development and the third and fourth chakras. The yoga for this root race unfoldment is Raja yoga.

Meruvian Race. Focused on the integration and synthesis of the first three root races and the opening of the intuitive function in humanity. The yoga for this race is Ashtanga and Agni yoga, which is also called fire yoga. The Meruvian race focuses on unfolding of the fifth and sixth chakras.

Paradisian Race. Focuses on the fulfillment of the divine plan for this particular planetary cycle. This race takes humanity to the full unfoldment of the crown chakra.

It must be understood that there is great overlapping between these five cycles or races, for they span over eleven million years of Earth's history. Advanced initiates are not limited by these root races. They have in the past and can in the future move far ahead of average humanity's development. I add that the term "Aryan race" as used by Adolph Hitler was a complete misuse of this divinely inspired term, and it is not what I am speaking of here.

This is obviously a vast subject, and this book is not an appropriate place for an in-depth study. However, the study of the races of humanity is fascinating, and one's ultimate understanding will shed further light as to where he/she is centered, which chakras within her are most active and how best to deal with her needs and evolutionary process.

My purpose in including this brief overview is to show you just how far reaching the true understanding of race is and to familiarize you with certain terms should you come across them in your studies. More than that, I hope that it will propel you directly into the broad Christ-mind interpretation of the matter. This way, the "problem" of the races will be elevated and integrated with the spiritual aspect of self. Once done, the solution to these difficulties will be most apparent.

The Healing and Integration within the Family Unit

Sometimes the issues that are closest to us and that appear the simplest are indeed the most difficult. The biological family unit is one of the best and most powerful examples.

The sensitive nature of both nuclear and extended families touches each of us deeply. Remember that when we arrived upon this Earth, our immediate families appeared to us as Gods. We were dependent upon the care of mother/father parents for absolutely everything. When we were hungry or thirsty, they were there with the wellspring of life's sustenance to feed us. When we were uncomfortable and cried out, it was they who made us comfortable. They had the power of giving, and withdrawing, love. They soothed and quieted our fears. And in some cases, they neglected us.

In this way we were indoctrinated into their belief system. Those parented by people lacking a more advanced psychological/spiritual nature of communicating find that a great deal of their adult lives is spent reprogramming their belief systems, so that they view the world by the light of the spiritual mind, rather than that of negative-ego belief systems. Many of us worked hard and diligently to reprogram our inappropriate behavioral responses, responses whose root patterns stem from childhood behavior learned as a means of survival.

An example of this survival behavior is a male child who, in order to earn the respect of a father, learns to not cry, because in that family structure to cry denotes weakness. Another family structure might thrive on the weakness and dependence of its children and family members. For example, the child in such a family who constantly gets colds subconsciously self-generates them to make the parents feel secure, and in turn is re-warded with the love he/she seeks.

The difficulty with these imbalanced family systems is when the child grows up, he/she learns that what worked within the nuclear family does not necessarily work in the greater world. In fact, the faulty belief patterns that gave the child the security he sought at home serves only to bring him great insecurity within the world. It is here that the process of separation from the family usually begins.

The Pulling-Away Period

The realization of the dysfunction of certain belief systems (which served the purpose of the child but now only hampers the development of the growing adult) often results in a pulling-away period where the adult child seeks to rebuild a new and healthier identity. This can be done by receiving psychological and/or spiritual counseling, or by rebelling and withdrawing from the family unit altogether. It is hoped that the young adult does this in as healthy and spiritual a means as possible by learning how to clear the negative ego within him/herself and likewise learning how to forgive.

It is not uncommon a definite period of pulling away from one's imme-diate family to ensure. As a stage this can be quite useful, for it allows the young adult to get a feeling for him/herself as an independent entity, rather than a mere extension of the family unit. It also allows him to con-nect with his own inner-plane and/or spiritual family, where the ties are generally stronger. The famous Swiss psychologist Carl Jung called this the process of individualization.

This period is not meant to last forever; although in certain extreme cases that might indeed be the healthiest of choices. It is the reintegration within the family as a whole to which one should strive. This should not be at the expense of one's own individual health and clarity; therefore, cer-tain boundaries need to be established—boundaries not built on any form of anger or negative-ego thinking. Ultimately, these boundaries should be established in a place of loving forgiveness, accepting the uniqueness of both oneself and one's family.

Inner- and Outer-Plane Forgiveness

The ultimate goal is finding true forgiveness for both self and family for behaviors that were dominant in the past. This would manifest in outer-plane forgiveness and a willingness to reintegrate within the family unit without crossing your own boundaries or allowing others to cross them. I realize this is the ideal, and this is how I hold it up to you.

There are certain unfortunate situations that involve a continuing pattern of abuse on the part of one or both parents, a sibling or other relative. If this is the case, the healing and integration must be done within yourself, because continuing to expose yourself to any physical or psychic abuse would most definitely not be recommended. There is no reason that any one of us should be subjected to abuse, even if that abuse comes from within the nuclear family itself.

Mastering your anger and readjusting your attitude to one of forgiveness might require much psychological and/or spiritual counseling. I am not saying you will not need to do some strictly psychological work (for you will indeed), but if the work is being done in the light of your higher self, then it truly becomes effective work and not just continual reinforcement of the lower self's reactions. The key is to find a counselor who embraces both the psychological and spiritual approach in his/her work. A strictly psychological approach can be helpful in the early stages of development, but will become increasingly less so as the disciple/initiate evolves. Traditional psychology does not yet recognize the need to transcend negative-ego thinking or that it is our thoughts that cause our realities. It might also serve to reinforce negative-ego thinking and behavior because of its faulty or limited philosophical understanding.

Working with such tools as those in *Soul Psychology* can build a strong God-centered foundation upon which to do any other kind of work. A book that I have found helpful is *A Course in Miracles*. The main point is, both on the outer plane and on the inner planes, strive to come to terms with who you are as an individual soul within the kingdom of spirit and truly learn how to forgive.

Journal-Processing for Forgiveness

One practical tool of forgiveness lies within easy reach of pen and paper. You can start by listing the person whom you find hardest to forgive. Next make a column stating the areas in which you are having the most trouble forgiving. Allow your inner child to express the hurts and betrayal in each of these various areas. Don't try to edit this with your conscious mind, but rather give this time fully to the uninhibited expression of the hurt child within.

When you feel as though that part of you has had its say, call forth your higher self/oversoul to express itself. The higher self or oversoul is the true adult and ultimate spiritual parent of forgiveness within you, so let it have its say. Allow the uninhibited expression of this most spiritual part of yourself to propel you past blame, anger, hurt and fear into the very heart of love and forgiveness itself. This part of you has never been harmed, for, as Krishna says in the sacred book of India, the Bhagavad-Gita, "not burned by fire, not wetted by water, birthless, deathless am I".

And so in that spiritual essence are you. It is easy for this aspect to forgive, for *it* has never been harmed.

Then allow your conscious mind to bring these two aspects together, so that you—the you functioning via the conscious mind—can use the power of the superconscious, higher self/oversoul to integrate its wisdom and act as guide until you are ultimately able to say, feel and demonstrate the word "forgive."

The Healing

The degree of healing will depend upon the depth of hurt and your own ability to trust the higher self within you. In a severe case, where perhaps both physical and emotional abuse were present, it might be absolutely appropriate that you never see that person again. This, however, should not stop the inner-plane healing and forgiveness from occurring. In truth, in order to move on, we all must ultimately heal and release the negative emotions that bind. That is why I promote forgiveness where even the worst of upbringings has occurred. To forgive is to clear away the negative emotions and thought forms that keep one a prisoner of the past. When you find that place of ultimate forgiveness, you have embraced a big piece of divinity, and can thence move forward.

When the wrongs that are forgiven are of a much lesser degree, you might feel yourself ready to see and/or rejoin your nuclear family or others in question. Much of this will depend upon who both you and they are now, what your value systems are and what the conditions of your interactions are. This is an area totally unique to each individual and to the individual family unit.

I remind you, however, that no matter how close you might be, hold firm to the boundaries you have set. Remember, you have done much work to come into your own, and no one should be allowed to invade that place of your own personal power. Family members, especially, are quick to try and reclaim the power they once had over you, so be vigilant to remain the psychologically balanced, integrated son/daughter of God that you know yourself to be.

Affirmations

- I'm integrated and whole within myself.
- I meet my family (or specific individual) and the world from a place of wholeness.
- I have forgiven the past and am therefore free.
- I embrace myself and my family (or specific individual) within the grace of forgiveness.

- I create my own boundaries and can therefore love safely.
- I am synthesized and whole within the family of God.
- I am the creator of my divine destiny of love.
- I see all people and situations with the eyes of the Christ/spiritual mind.
- I release all fears and blockages from the past and move forward to claim my divine heritage.
- I and my Father/Mother God are one.

Integrating Our Individual Rays and Astrological Signs

There are many forces at play within us. Some obvious ones are the psychological forces that shaped us as children, which we are now endeavoring to reshape with the help of our higher selves and Christ consciousness. We likewise bear the mark of our particular race, creed, nation and even the city and state where we reside.

We also brought forth the type of physical/etheric, astral, emotional and mental/psychological bodies that we created in past incarnations. Each of us was born under various heavenly configurations and have an astrological chart and pattern unique unto itself.

The Rays

Moving more into the abstract sciences, likewise we each have a particular ray and energy stream that are at play within us. The science of the rays is a relatively new one, although it is founded upon an ancient and eternal truth.

There was never a time when we were not affected by the rays. However, the study of the part they play in our lives is recent. A brief description of the rays, their qualities and the various masters or chohans of the rays was given earlier and therefore need not be repeated here. It is worthy to note, however, that our bodies fall under the influence of various rays and their specific energies, and this, in turn, is added to our complex makeup.

For example, if your personality aspect is under the influence of the first, or will, ray, that would give you a very forceful personality. If you were born under one of the fire signs of the zodiac, that would add fire to fire, so to speak. If, however, you were at the point on your path of initiation where you were highly influenced by the higher self or oversoul and that was located on the sixth ray of devotion, you would then have quite an interesting mixture of energies—devotion, will and power/fire. Add to that the influence of the planets and the fact that the rays affect each of the various bodies by their own unique energy pattern, and the complex picture of a human being becomes apparent. It is important to realize that although the rays, astrological influences, inherited traits, past-life programming, upbringing, environment and planetary forces all influence each person, the strongest influence is personal power aligned with free choice. And this should never be forgotten.

It is not the purpose of this book to make the simple complex, but rather to simplify the complicated. Therefore, I bring all this to your attention that you may be aware of two things: First, humanity is a microcosm of the macrocosm of God itself, and not the simple accident of nature many a scientist would have you believe; and second, synthesis and integration of the components that contribute to the complete expression of you will empower you with understanding. Finding out your basic soul/monadic ray will greatly aid in the understanding of yourself. Although it is obviously not the complete picture, such knowledge can greatly aid you in understanding how you perceive the world and your place in it. It is much like knowing your sun sign and astrological chart and the great influence that wields (along with your own free will, of course.) A qualified channeler could help integrate this information for you and perhaps even break down the effects of the rays upon the different bodies. This would not be unlike consulting a qualified astrologer.

Another point I wish to address is the relationship between your particular initiation level and the ray of your higher self. Just as the signs of the zodiac have a higher and lower expression, so do the rays. Much of this I explained in detail in *The Complete Ascension Manual*. The point I make here is that if you are well on your way upon the path of initiation and ascension, the ray that will dominate is that of your higher self, and then, a bit further along, that of your monad.

Once you find out which level you are at and which ray either your higher self and/or monad is on, you can then use that information to call upon the higher self and/or monad and the attendant ray to harmonize and synthesize the whole, thus bringing into balance your entire four-body system. Not only will you bring it into balance, but you will invoke the highest aspect of yourself to accomplish this.

This is but a tiny piece of a vast subject—one I believe you will find interesting. If you feel so inclined, I've suggested a variety of ways to work with the rays and their attributes in *The Complete Ascension Manual*. For our discussion here, I encourage you to find out what ray you are on at the higher self and/or monad level so that you can then work with the energies. This will enable you to do so with a clarity that would not otherwise be available to you. You may contact me at the telephone number at the back of this book if you would like me to recommend a qualified channeler to help you. The more tools you have to work with, the faster and easier your work will be.

Personal Integration

Seeking personal integration requires utmost honesty and acquiring as much information about ourselves as we possibly can. It likewise requires total acceptance of who we are and unconditional love for ourselves.

Once we are able to accept ourselves and unconditionally love ourselves, then the work of integration and synthesis can truly begin. If, however, you find yourself unable to manifest self-love, please do work on that area. The quality of unconditional self-love must be brought forth within each and every one of us. "Know ye not that ye are sons and daughters of the most High"? This quality is vital and is our divine birthright and heritage.

Don't be afraid to look within the furthest reaches of yourself. Don't be afraid to get up real close either. Each of the four lower bodies, from the physical through the higher mental, constitute who we are this lifetime. Likewise do our higher bodies, and that is why the higher we can see through the inner spiritual eye, the better. Incorporate *all* that is known by all information acquired. Don't try to disavow your race, sex, religious background or even the color of your hair. Look at everything through eyes that observe without attachment. Acquire all that you can regarding the rays and astrological influences in your lives, as well as that contained within any other area of mundane or occult study that suits you. Then sit and focus on the highest possible aspect of yourself and set the intent for integration.

Tools for Self-Integration & Creating Your Physical Body

Integration Journal and Affirmation List
for the Physical Self

Begin by listing the physical qualities about yourself that have most disturbed you. Create the list on one side of the page. The following is a sample list.

1. Not pretty/handsome enough
2. Awkward gait in my walk
3. Nose too big/small
4. Too short/tall
5. Have terrible hair
6. Much too thin/fat
7. Teeth are crooked

Take a hard look at the list you have made, and make sure that it is complete. If it is, then rewrite the list in the descending order from the aspect of your physical appearance you find most disturbing down through least disturbing until the list is complete.

Draw a line down the middle of the page, and on the right side write down the polar opposite of your negative-ego reactions to your physical body. List them in the unconditionally self-loving and embracing point of view of your higher self and Christ mind. The sample list might then read as follows.

1. Not pretty/handsome	I. I am beautiful in the sight of God.
2. Awkward gait in my walk	II. My walk flows in perfect rhythm with the universe as it is.
3. Nose too big/small	III. My nose is the perfect size as it is.
4. Too short/tall	IV. I am the perfect height to express my individuality.
5. Have terrible hair	V. I have the perfect hair for me.
6. Much too fat/thin	VI. I am the perfect weight at this moment in God's time.
7. Teeth are crooked	VII. My teeth are perfect as they are.

Silently read the statements about the aspects of yourself that you dislike, and then proceed to read aloud the positive affirmations you have written from your higher self and Christ mind. Then on a separate piece of paper, just write down the positive affirmations, and repeat them a couple of times. This is the science of attitudinal healing and of positive affirmations.

Understanding and Application of Journal and List

The point of this exercise is not that you must continue to live with those physical characteristics that are within your power to change to ones more compatible with your inner vision of yourself. The point is that before things change, we must allow ourselves to accept and embrace them for what they are in God's eyes—not just in our negative ego and what it has taught us. Once this is done, you have freed yourself from any negative attachments and have the true freedom to effectuate change in the appropriate areas.

For example, most of us have the power to alter our body weight by regular exercise and changing our eating patterns. But it is essential to begin by knowing that the excess weight served as a teacher in some regard and to honor that. If we have been overweight most of our lives, perhaps it has been out of a desire to insulate ourselves from the world. There was a definite purpose for this state of being. There is actually a lesson in everything; the trick is to find the lesson and move on. It is also self-defeating to compare our weight to negative-ego ideals that permeate magazines, television and movies. Happiness is a state of mind, not a state of weight.

If you are very tall or very small and are uncomfortable with that fact, why not focus on the lesson that is inherent in your being the way you are, since height is not readily changed through any physical means other than wearing lifts or high heels—or wearing flat shoes instead of elevated ones. Whenever you find yourself stuck in a situation that will most likely last your entire incarnation, it is always a good practice to journal-write about it and see what comes up for you. In areas such as the above example, you can create a multitude of affirmations, changing the way you view your particular situation. I call this the making-lemonade out-of-lemons-lesson initiation. There is always good in any situation waiting to be freed by the power of your spiritual mind, much the way the statues of Michelangelo waited to be freed by his chisel from the block of marble that encased them. The spiritual mind focuses on what it can do, not on what it can't. This is related to living out the puzzle piece God has given you and not trying to live out someone else's puzzle piece.

There are other areas within your physical appearance that need close examination before deciding what to do. One of the better examples of this would be "to nose-job, or not to nose-job?" New Age lightworkers are naturalists and would never think of doing this in a million years. However, this certainly does not apply to everyone and might not apply in your case. While tending to live more as the naturalist, I basically have an open mind on matters like this. I believe that the decision should be based on a clear understanding of what you are doing and, most important, why? Are you trying to keep up with someone else and feel you need to alter your looks to fit into an image that you don't believe in anyway? Or, on the other hand, do you truly feel that such a change will uplift your spirits and bring you into better harmony with yourself? If this is the case, I say go for it. As Buddha said, "Walk the middle way," and it is up to each of us to determine what that point of balance is within ourselves. If we do that from as honest and spiritually aligned a place as possible, then we are doing what, for us, is right. Cosmetic surgery, in and of itself, is neutral. The key question is whether the motivation stems from the negative ego (false vanity) or from the higher self and oversoul, which sees some divine purpose for taking such a step. The key in all such matters is intent and motivation.

Emotional-Body Integration

The tools offered for the physical body can also be used for integrating the emotional and mental bodies. You can create a similar list relating to your astral/emotional body and another one relating to your mental body.

Journal Affirmation List for the Emotional Self.

1. Overly sensitive
2. Too quick to anger
3. Too shut down

Then follow the format given for the physical body and draw a line down the center of the page listing the affirmations that counter the ones you just wrote. For example:

1. Overly sensitive
    I. I am balanced within myself and I act rather than react.

2. Too quick to anger
    II. I am calm and placid as a quiet, peaceful pond.

3. Too shut down
    III. While keeping my boundaries, I open like a flower in spring.

Reread the guidance given for the physical body, only this time apply it to your emotional self. You can definitely create change there, as long as you remember that it lies within your choice whether or not you want to stay stuck in a specific groove of feeling or open to the heart of your higher self and learn what it is like just to be in a state of unconditional love. If you are experiencing extreme blocks and difficulties, you also have the choice to find a qualified psychologist or spiritual counselor to help you work through major difficulties. One choice we often forget is the choice to ask for help. There are certainly situations that call for this. Therefore, please know that just as the masters are available to help you on the inner planes, so too are well-trained initiates in the healing arts there to help you here on Earth. Please, beloved readers, do not think it is a sign of weakness to ask for help. That simply is not so. To ask for help when help is needed is one of the strongest and smartest things a person can do for him/herself.

Never forget that your higher self and/or monad are there, as are the masters, simply awaiting an invitation to help you with total love and a blending of divine purpose. For in truth, you are one. Diligent and focused work in this attitudinal healing-and-affirmation process, over time, will completely reprogram the subconscious and conscious minds to the point that they perfectly reflect the programming of the superconscious mind and higher self. When this is achieved, a continual state of inner peace, even-mindedness, unconditional love, forgiveness, joy, happiness and even bliss can be maintained. For how we feel does not come from the outer world but from how we *interpret* the outer world. We can't always control what happens in our outer lives, but we can control how we choose to think about those events. Thinking with the negative-ego mind creates anger, impatience, frustration, anxiety, depression, sadness and disappointment. Thinking with the Christ mind creates just the opposite—looking at a given situation as a teaching/lesson/challenge. It is all how you look at it. The ideal is to look for the silver lining in every dark cloud.

Mental-Body Integration

For brevity's sake, now that you have grown familiar with the type of lists we are talking about, I will combine both the quality you might be working to overcome and the one you will be seeking to replace it with in the same list. The following is an example of the second stage of creating your affirmation list for mental healing.

Journal & Affirmation List for the Mental Self

1. Always pessimistic   I.   I am always optimistic.
2. Always judge others   II.   I accept and love others.
3. Hate this job   III.   I bless this job.

Again, follow a similar process of working with this mental body as you did with the physical and emotional. Thoughts are basically habit and habits can be created or broken within a twenty-one-day period. We are not trapped by our thoughts. What we generally do, however, is create thoughts that trap us. This really is just a bad habit that can be changed by replacing faulty thinking with thinking via the Christ/spiritual mind.

Thoughts are of a more refined nature than that of dense matter. Therefore, the etheric and even the emotional/astral planes are much more pliable. The two things required are: first, learning to think with the Christ mind ("Let this mind be in you as was in Christ Jesus"); and second, the use of will. The power of will can be harnessed to will ourselves to do daily affirmations. These can be done either silently or aloud; however, the practice must be consistent. The will cans also be used to deny the entrance of negative thoughts into our conscious minds. This can be likened to a plant that is not being watered and therefore it withers and dies. The positive affirmation is the new seed-thought that is planted in the receptive soil of the subconscious mind and begins to sprout and grow with watering. Metaphorically, this is the constant repetition of the new positive affirmation for twenty-one days. We likewise can use the will by choosing to surround ourselves with people of Christ consciousness, by not allowing indulgence in negative thought patterns when we find that they are coming into play and by being willing to make the necessary changes in our thought worlds.

As with all four lower bodies, the mental body has the capacity to be infused with divine light, allowing the inflow of higher energies to shift the thought process to a higher vibration. In essence, the idea is to integrate and synthesize the bodies within themselves and then with each other, so that we, as an enlightened and integrated whole, may function as gods and goddesses upon the Earth.

Total-Body Alignment & Integration Meditation

Find a comfortable chair or a comfortable position lying down, with back straight and arms and legs uncrossed, unless in yoga posture.

Take a full deep breath into the physical body.

Exhale, releasing all physical toxins and inharmonious energies.

Relax for about a minute, feeling the natural flow of the breath.

Take a full deep breath into the etheric body.

Exhale, releasing all etheric toxins and inharmonious energies.

Relax a moment, feeling the natural flow of the breath.

Take a full deep breath into your astral or feeling/emotional body.

Exhale, releasing all emotional toxins and inharmonious energies.

Relax a moment, feeling the natural flow of the breath.

Take a full deep breath into your mental body.

Exhale, releasing all negative thought patterns, toxins and inharmonious energies.

Relax a moment, feeling the natural flow of the breath.

Take a full deep breath, aligning all four lower bodies.

Exhale, feeling all bodies coming into alignment and integration with one another.

Follow the natural flow of the breath while visualizing the alignment and integration of each of the bodies within themselves and with each other.

After a few minutes, take another deep breath and call upon your higher self.

Ask your higher self to come into full alignment with your four lower bodies and to radiate its divine love and light upon them.

Exhale, and feel the presence of your higher self as it aligns, blesses and integrates within the four-body system.

Relax a moment, feeling the natural flow of the breath.

Take another deep breath and call upon your monad.

Ask your monad to come into full alignment with your higher self and four lower bodies and to radiate its divine light, love and power upon them.

Exhale, and feel the presence of your monad, your own mighty I Am Presence, as it aligns, blesses and integrates with all other aspects of self.

Relax, following the in-and-out flow of the breath, and simply enjoy this divine state of integration and alignment.

Stay in meditation for as long as is comfortable, using the mantra, "God and I are one and are integrated on all possible levels."

If you are new to this type of meditation I would advise to give yourself at most ten to fifteen minutes for about a month, gradually building up to a forty-minute-meditation period.

I believe in moderation in all things and following the middle path. Your bodies will need time to adjust to the flow of energies that are coming in through this type of meditation, so go about it slowly and peacefully. I'm not one to place bets, but if I were I'd bet on the tortoise rather than the hare anytime.

When you are ready to come out of meditation, visualize a grounding cord extending all the way from your mighty I Am Presence to about a foot underneath the Earth. Establish yourself firmly grounded, aligned, integrated and linked to and with the Earth.

When this is done, give thanks to God, the masters, your monad, higher self and all the various bodies that meditated with you.

Slowly get up and go about your day as a fully aligned and integrated whole.

Concluding Thoughts on Self-Integration

The more integrated with self we become, the faster and safer our spiritual journeys will be. The path of ascension takes all bodies into consideration and requires a cleansing and purifying, accelerating and aligning them into one fully awakened, functioning whole. Once we are whole within ourselves, once we are integrated and synthesized within ourselves, then it becomes so much simpler and more enjoyable to discover, integrate and effectuate our particular puzzle piece within the world.

Some of us are more mental types while others are more emotional, still others more artistic and so on. The most important point is that we each come to the perfect place of balance within ourselves. It is fine to be more of one type than another. In fact, our differences are an integral part of the divine plan. What is not part of the divine plan, however, is that we ascend in *fragments*.

Many advanced initiates find that they are stumbling over mole hills, which, in essence, are fragments of themselves that they thought they could get around by virtue of their ascension process. This is not the way things work. The ultimate requirement for progressing into the higher stages of ascension is integrating, cleansing, clearing and synthesizing every single part of our selves. Therefore, to you beginners, I ask you to welcome the grace of these teachings, for you are learning the easy way rather than the harder way.

Sometimes it gets very tempting to say, "Well, the physical body can be a real drag and since I know I'm not really the body, I'll just pretend I don't have one and ignore it." Sound familiar? It certainly looks all right on paper. But this is not the way it works. It does not work for the physical body, the feeling body or the mental body.

What we are meant to do with these bodies is to get them vibrating at the highest possible frequency, raise the light and love quotients within each of the bodies, align with the higher self and/or monad and then step down the divine energies contained in these higher aspects of ourselves and in a synthesized manner ground them upon the Earth. The phrase, "All is God and that I am," which so many lightworkers speak, is indeed truth. Since it is truth, it therefore follows that their path of the whole includes the whole. It is with utter love that I say to you, relax, and enjoy the process. For, indeed, *the path is the goal.* Our path leads to ever-deeper wisdom, love and blending with the whole, and that is why we are on it.

Synthesis and integration are both the key and the door we unlock. With that understanding, I ask you to pay as much attention to this process as you can. Work with the tools given in this chapter, as well as the others I have mentioned and those that you come up with yourselves. The paths of initiation/ascension and integration/synthesis are truly one and the same. Walk the path in this light and I assure you, your footing will be secure.

About the Author

Joshua David Stone has a Ph.D. in transpersonal psychology and is a licensed marriage, family and child counselor in Los Angeles, California. On a spiritual level, he anchors the Melchizedek Synthesis Light Academy and Ashram, which is an integrated inner- and outer-plane ashram representing all paths to God. Serving as a spokesperson for the planetary ascension movement, Stone's spiritual lineage is directly linked to Djwhal Khul, Sananda, Kuthumi, Lord Maitreya, Lord Melchizedek, the Mahatma and Metatron. He also feels a close connection with the Divine Mother and Lord Buddha, as well as a deep devotion to Sathya Sai Baba.

Contact Joshua David Stone, Ph.D. at:
5252 Coldwater Canyon Ave., #112
Van Nuys, CA 91401
(818) 769-1181
Fax: (818) 766-1782

About the Author

Rev. Janna Shelley Parker is a longtime initiate of the ascended master Djwhal Khul and a past student of Hilda Charlton. Rev. Parker works as Stone's personal assistant in the Melchizedek Synthesis Light Ashram in Los Angeles, which serves Lord Melchizedek, the Mahatma, Metatron, Sai Baba, Lord Buddha, Lord Maitreya and Djwhal Khul. She teaches yoga and journal-channeling and writes poetry and song lyrics.

Other books by Joshua David Stone, Ph.D., published by Light Technology

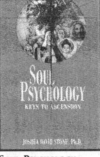

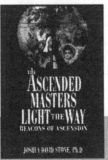

A Beginner's Guide to the Path of Ascension
This volume covers the basics of ascension clearly and completely, from the spiritual hierarchy to the angels and star beings.
ISBN 1-891824-02-3

Golden Keys to Ascension and Healing — Revelations of Sai Baba and the Ascended Masters
This book represents the wisdom of the ascended masters condensed into concise keys that serve as a spiritual guide. These 420 golden keys present the multitude of insights Dr. Stone has gleaned from his own background and his path to God realization.
ISBN 1-891824-03-1

Manual for Planetary Leadership
Here at last is an indispensible book that has been urgently needed in these uncertain times. It lays out the guidelines for leadership in the world and in one's life. It serves as a reference manual for moral and spiritual living.
ISBN 1-891824-05-8

Your Ascension Mission — Embracing Your Puzzle Piece
This book shows how each person's puzzle piece is just as vital and necessary as any other. All aspects of living the fullest expression of your individuality.
ISBN 1-891824-09-0

Revelations of a Melchizedek Initiate
Dr. Stone's spiritual autobiography, beginning with his ascension initiation and progression into the 12th initiation. Filled with insight, tools and information.
ISBN 1-891824-10-4

How to Teach Ascension Classes
This book serves as an ideal foundation for teaching ascension classes and presenting workshops. It covers an entire one- to two-year program of classes.
ISBN 1-891824-15-5

$14.95 EACH

Ascension and Romantic Relationships
Inspired by Djwhal Khul, Dr. Stone has written a unique book about relationships from the perspective of the soul and monad rather than just the personality. This presents a broader picture of the problems and common traps of romantic relationships and offers much deeper advice.
ISBN 1-891824-16-3